# TELLING STORIES, WRITING LIVES:
## A Handbook for Beginning Adult Writers

Bird Stasz Ed. D

Matthew D. Adams

CAMBRIDGE Adult Education

REGENTS/PRENTICE HALL, Englewood Cliffs, New Jersey 07632

**Library of Congress Cataloging-in-Publication Data**

Stasz, Bird.
    Telling stories, writing lives : a handbook for beginning adult
  writers / Bird Stasz, Matthew D. Adams.
       p.  cm.
    ISBN 0-13-501123-X
    1. English language—Composition and exercises—Study and
teaching.   2. English language—Examinations—Study guides.
3. General educational development tests—Study guides.  I. Adams,
Matthew D.  II. Title.
LB1576.S782   1993
808'.042—dc20                              92-36801
                                          CIP

Acquisitions Editor: Mark Moscowitz
Editorial/production supervision and interior design: Cheryl Smith Robbins
Cover design: K&M Design
Prepress buyer: Ray Keating
Manufacturing buyer: Lori Bulwin
Interior artist: BM Graphics
Copy editor: Anne Graydon

 © 1993 by REGENTS/PRENTICE HALL
A Division of Simon & Schuster
Englewood Cliffs, New Jersey 07632

Printed in the United States of America

10 9 8 7 6 5 4 3 2

ISBN 0-13-501123-X

Prentice-Hall International (UK) Limited, *London*
Prentice-Hall of Australia Pty. Limited, *Sydney*
Prentice-Hall Canada Inc., *Toronto*
Prentice-Hall Hispanomericana, S.A., *Mexico*
Prentice-Hall of India Private Limited, *New Delhi*
Prentice-Hall of Japan, Inc., *Tokyo*
Simon & Schuster Asia Pte. Ltd., *Singapore*
Editora Prentice-Hall do Brasil, Ltda., *Rio de Janeiro*

# In Memorium

Carl Lewis Epperson 1929–1985

Margaret E. Champaigne 1950–1989

This book is lovingly dedicated
to their lives and their work.

*—Bird*

# Contents

*Acknowledgments ix*

## *Unit I    Getting Started:*
## *The Beginnings of Writing  1*

# *Unit II    Telling Stories: Personal Narrative 14*

# *Unit III    Answering Questions: Expository Writing 49*

# *Unit IV    Voices Rising: Persuasive Writing 64*

# Unit V   Easing into Essays: Writing for the GED and Other Situations  87

# Epilogue  101

# *Acknowledgments*

No matter how humble this book may appear, it could not have been done without countless hours contributed by many people other than the authors. First and foremost, we would like to thank Joshua Hertel for his valuable contributions to the creation of this book, especially the Expository Section. Josh not only contributed time, energy, and effort, but also lent support and vision. To him we are truly indebted. We would also like to thank Charles Temple for his invaluable advice; Lee Skrzyniarz for putting up with more than she had to; Mary Anne Wesse-Felter for reading too many drafts of this book; Robert Brunell for his wisdom; Mark Moscowitz for seeing it through; and Jim Brown for giving us a chance. In addition, an unsung hero in our literacy activities has been Andrew Furst—thanks!

—Bird and Matt

My personal thanks goes to my family for instilling the joy of reading in me and the "gang" for whatever it is they do. Thanks to Birdlet for everything.

—Matt

# Unit I

# Getting Started: The Beginnings of Writing

## WELCOMING LETTER (OR WHAT THIS BOOK IS ABOUT)

Hello!

Okay, we admit this may look like an ordinary textbook at first glance, but it is not. In a book like this, there are no lessons that you copy or tear out. You don't turn your work in for a grade. In fact, there are no grades. There are lots of writing exercises, some questions for you to answer, and some grammar exercises.

Grammar and punctuation are always scary because English has so many rules. We don't try to cover all of them. Instead, we have picked out some basic rules that we think will help you the most.

The point of this book is to help you write better in your everyday life. For some people this may mean taking a writing test, such as the GED. This book should help you get ready to write your GED essay, if that is your goal. We have included questions that are like those found on the GED, some practice essays, and some hints on how to take tests.

This book will also help you get ready to write essays in other kinds of situations, such as in community college. We have included questions that you might find on a community college placement test or on another kind of exam. There are some practice essays as well as some things to look for when you are reading essay test questions.

# HOW TO USE THIS BOOK

This book needs your cooperation. *Telling Stories, Writing Lives* will not work if you just sit there, turning the pages and reading the exercises. If you use this book correctly, you'll write a lot. The more you write, the better writer you will become. You'll need a writing notebook. A tablet of paper that you can keep in a folder is fine. It is important that you keep all of your writing in one place. Part of learning to be a better writer is learning how to edit or rewrite. Being able to look at your writing from time to time helps you understand your weaknesses and build on your strengths. At the end of the book it will be fun to be able to look back and see how far you've come.

You will find a number of exercises marked "journal." These entries are for you and do not need to be shown to anybody. We suggest you keep your journal in your writing notebook with your other work. Journal entries are a good way of getting more writing practice. Good writers, like good athletes, or good musicians, practice every day. The journal is one easy way to do that.

There are five units in the book. The units should be done in order. Each unit gets a little harder than the one before. All of the units have lots of writing exercises, but you don't need to do all of them. Do only as many as you feel you need (plus one or two more, just for good measure). Each of the sections has a number of grammar exercises. Remember, all of the grammar rules in this book are basic to becoming a better writer.

There are a few other things before we start. We set this book up as if you were in one of our writing workshops. With that in mind, you'll find that many of the writing exercises are about you. As a result, you are the expert.

As in our workshops, we recommend that you read a lot of your writing out loud to yourself and to other people. Sharing your writing with others gives you a chance to get some feedback. Feedback is how you learn if what you are writing is clear.

We also ask you to work with partners if possible. The more you work with others and the more you talk about your writing, the better writer you will become. We will ask you to do more than one draft of your work. That is simply what authors do. It's rare that even the very best of writers writes perfectly the first time out. Drafts are not a big deal. They give you a chance to fiddle with ideas, phrases, and words just to see how they sound.

The final thing is that, believe it or not, this should be fun. We're putting you in great hands—yours. So, find some paper, a pencil, and maybe even a partner and get started!

Best Wishes,
*Bird and Matt*

# LET LOOSE AND WRITE

All right, before we start writing, let's take a look at what this writing business is all about.

What does writing mean to you? How do you see yourself as a writer?

It's important to check in with yourself and understand what you believe about something before you get going.

First we will have a quiz—just kidding!

To get a sense of how you feel about writing, take a look at these questions, number your paper, and answer them *true* or *false.* There are no right or wrong answers here, so fire away!

1. Writing helps me solve my problems.
2. Writing makes me feel stupid.
3. Writing is a very powerful tool.
4. Writing is for nerds.
5. Writing has too many rules.
6. I don't really need to write.
7. I would like to write more.
8. I don't really want to write; I just want to pass my GED.
9. Writing will help my reading.
10. If I write better, I will be more independent.
11. Writing is too hard to be worth it.
12. Writing is my life.
13. If I learn to write better, I might be able to get a better job.
14. I hate to spell.
15. Punctuation is hard.
16. Punctuation is easy.

Look back at how you answered these questions. Jot down how you see yourself as a writer. If you don't really know, then mark the statements that best describe how you feel about writing.

Are your thoughts positive or negative?
If positive, what are your strengths?
If negative, what are your weaknesses?
What's the thing about writing that worries you the most?

If possible, find someone else to look over these questions and compare answers (different strokes for different folks).

Even though everyone may feel different about writing, many (or maybe even most) people suffer from what is called "writing anxiety." In other words, many people are afraid of putting words on a page. Lots of times they go to great effort to avoid writing. Folks make pots of coffee, search for hours to find their favorite pencil, clean the dust balls out from under the beds—anything, but put words on paper.

Most of the time people do all these things because they are afraid, afraid that they will be wrong or sound silly. Too often people are worried that what they write is "wrong" or "not good." Rules of writing scare people. Well, for now, let us not worry so much about rules. Just forget about them for a few minutes.

Sometimes, though, all that wandering around is a way of thinking with "the backside of your brain." Even as you do all of this stuff, your mind is thinking about what you might write. Learn to listen to that voice.

Writing is scary because it often makes you put yourself down on paper for all the world to see. That's risky business. However, when you feel comfortable (or even almost comfortable), share your writing with someone else. Bouncing ideas off of one another is a great way to become a better writer. Remember the old saying: "Two heads are better than one." That really applies to writing.

## Introduction to Freewriting

One way to cure writing anxiety is to do an exercise called *freewriting*. Freewriting is simply writing privately for a few minutes about anything you want. It is writing with the "backside of your mind." You should *not* worry about spelling (make it up if you want), or grammar, or even making sense. You don't have to share it with anybody. All you want to do is write. If you can't think of anything to write, then write your name over and over.

** Freewrite for ten minutes. **

You can write on *anything* you want, or you can try these ideas:

1. Write about your shirt.
2. Write about your desk.
3. Write about "freewriting."
4. Write about the sounds in the room.
5. Write about your breakfast.
6. Write about your pet's breath.
7. Write about your family.
8. Write about your future.
9. Write about the inside of a pencil sharpener.
10. Write a paragraph of random words.

Now take a look at what you wrote. Read it to yourself. Did you cheat and worry about rules? It's okay to use "standard" grammar and spelling, but it isn't okay to worry about it.

> ## Reflections
>
> What kinds of things happened as you wrote? Sometimes when people freewrite they realize that one story grows out of another one. That's fine.
>
> Did you hear a voice in your head telling you what a crummy writer you are? We used to hear that voice a lot. When you write, especially in freewriting, you need to tell that voice to BE QUIET!
>
> Let's try another exercise.

Freewrite for ten minutes on anything you want.

OR

Go back to the list and pick another topic.

OR

Write about something in your pocket.

REMEMBER don't stop writing to correct mistakes.

We will be using the power of freewriting throughout the whole book. Remember, freewriting is supposed to be "free" of worrying about mistakes or corrections. It is the best way we know of to get you warmed up and writing.

# THE WRITING PROCESS IN A NUTSHELL

And because I found I had nothing else to write about, I presented myself as a subject.

*—Montaigne*

We're sure that you will find many interesting and exciting things to write about. If you're feeling dry on ideas though, one never-ending interesting subject is yourself (your family, your home, your friends).

But what if you are feeling dry about organizing your ideas? In the next few pages, we will look at some ways to shape and organize your writing.

The first thing we look at is the five-step writing process. This is an easy and fun way to begin writing. As in making a cake or building a fire, you follow certain steps and, TA-DA!, you have a nice tidy paragraph.

Normally, it is best to write with other people. For now, though, let us be your partner. We will be talking you through this process (using Bird's lists). Our thoughts will be written in boxes, so you will be able to tell when we are thinking aloud.

Writing is both *process* and **product.** *Process* is the act of writing. Peter Elbow describes it as "cooking and growing." *Process* takes time and comes with practice. *Product* is what you have at the end: the paragraph, the page, the letter, the short story, the poem. Product comes when you are clear on what you want to say and you can say it clearly. The five-step writing process is just one way to help you get started. Remember that good writers learn to be good writers by writing a lot.

You need five pieces of paper. Label them 1–5.

## Okay, STEP ONE—Sheet One

On the first piece of paper, make a list of four things you might want to write about. RELAX. These can be anything: from Fluffy the cat, to the day that your alarm clock was struck by lightning. Think of things that are close to you. Think of things that make you laugh or cry. Think about people and places you love. Think about good food and fun times. Just make a list!

Remember that this is MY list. YOUR list should have things that only you know about.

- My cat
- My son putting his dad's underpants in the toaster oven
- My sister stopping traffic
- My home in Puerto Rico

Look at your list of topics and ask yourself some questions.

Which one would you want to talk about most?
What would you say?
Who would you talk to?
Which topic feels the best?
Which one seems to be the easiest and most fun?
Take your pick and circle it.

This is an example of how Bird thought as she chose her topic:

*My Cat:* He's not all that interesting and I don't know what I would say about him anyway.
*My Son:* He is very funny. I know a lot about him. This would be an easy topic to write about.
*My Sister:* She is very funny also, but she might not want me to write about her.
*My Old Home:* That topic is too sad and it makes me homesick.

## STEP TWO—Sheet Two

Write your chosen topic on the top of the second sheet of paper. Now begin to jot down phrases, words, sights, sounds, and smells about your topic. Sometimes it helps to close your eyes for a minute and really think hard about the topic. Try to get a photograph in your mind of who or what you are writing about. Look at your list again and ask yourself some questions.

- What words bring pictures to your mind?
- What seems to be missing?

This is a list of Bird's ideas and phrases for her paragraph:

My son putting his father's underpants in the toaster oven.

He was three years old.
The underpants were wet.
The smoke alarm went off.
The underpants caught fire.
He began to cry.
It was in the afternoon.
The toaster is old.
I was upstairs.

## STEP THREE—Sheet Three:
## First Draft

This is easy! Take the ideas on sheet two and put them together. For right now, don't worry about spelling, periods, or any of those things. Don't fret about the order or the way that it looks. Just write it down!

Once you are done, find someone to read your paragraph out loud to, or read it out loud to yourself. Reading aloud is important because you need to hear how your work sounds. Reading aloud will help you make your writing better.

This is what Bird's first draft looks like:

The Day My Son Put His Dad's Underpants in the Toaster Oven

He  was three and wearing red sleeper p.j.'s then the smoke alarm went off. The underpants caught fire and he began to cry. It was afternoon the toaster is old. I was upstairs when it happened.

## STEP FOUR—Sheet Four:
## Revising Your Work

After you've read your first draft, ask yourself these questions:

- What did you like the best?
- What do you want to know more about?
- What seems to be missing?
- Does your draft make sense?
- This is where you would fix your grammar, punctuation, and spelling. (We will worry about this later).

Bird's reflections on her piece: "Overall it's not too bad but the order isn't quite right, and I want to say more about the smoke."

## STEP FIVE—Sheet Five:
## Final Draft

Now that you have made all these changes, write your paragraph for the last time. Whew!

### The Day My Son Put His Dad's Underwear in the Oven

I was upstairs when I heard the fire alarm go off. I ran downstairs and found my three year old son, dressed in his red sleeper p.j.'s, crying. I looked and saw that he had put his dad's wet underpants in the toaster oven. He probably thought that they would dry. Instead, they were on fire. It is funny to think about it now, but at the time, it was a scary afternoon.

Great! CONGRATULATIONS! You have just finished your first piece of writing. See if you can get together with a partner and compare how you each developed your idea(s).

The five-step writing process can be really helpful to get your ideas started and your writing flowing. Please come back and do this process again whenever you feel the need.

## WRITER'S TOOL BOX

### Mapping

One of the keys to writing well is organization. We have outlined and practiced the five-step writing process. However, there are other ways to "get organized." One technique is called mapping. In mapping, a single word, idea, or phrase is placed in a circle in the center of the paper. Ideas, words, or phrases that have to do with the word in the center are put on lines that radiate from the circle. For example, Figure 1 shows how I used mapping to organize a piece about my favorite dog:

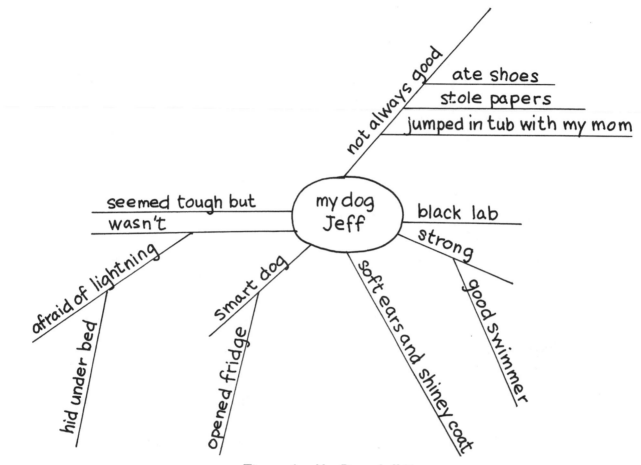

Figure 1. My-Dog-Jeff Map

---

## Writing Exercise

The mapping technique helps you order your thoughts and write. Using our example, try to write a descriptive piece entitled My Dog Jeff. Once you have written yours, compare it to ours:

### My Dog Jeff

My black lab was named Jeff. He was a strong dog and a good swimmer. His ears were soft and his coat was shiny. Jeff was fast. He could beat almost any other dog. Although he seemed tough he really wasn't. Jeff was afraid of lightning and always hid under the bed during thunderstorms. He was a very smart dog. As a puppy, he learned how to open doors, including the door to the fridge. Jeff was not always very good. He ate shoes and stole newspapers. Most of all, he liked to sneak into the bathroom and jump into the tub with my mom.

We will ask you to reflect on your work throughout the book. Reflections can be lots of things, but mostly they have to do with thinking about your work. To help you do that, we will ask many kinds of questions. Try to answer them as best as you can and remember that, for the most part, there isn't a right or wrong answer.

---

## Reflections

How is your piece like ours?
How is it different?

---

## Writing Exercise

Practice mapping. This time write about coming to class or about a friend. Before you begin writing, draw a map like the one in our example. Include as many images, events, sights, and sounds as you can. Write your piece from your map.

## Reflections

Read your piece out loud to yourself. Is there anything you might want to change? What do you like most about your piece? What do you think would make it clearer? Those changes are part of the editing process, which we will tell you about later. For now, just practice writing.

---

## Paragraphs and Details

So far most of the exercises in this book have asked you to write paragraphs. Paragraphs are the backbone of writing and, therefore, we need to spend a little more time just working on them.

In a nutshell, a *paragraph* is a group of related sentences about one topic or idea. A paragraph usually is made up of a topic sentence and supporting details. The writer begins the paragraph with a general statement, which is followed by details that make the statement clearer. Sometimes the last sentence in a paragraph is a wrap-up that brings the reader back to the general point. Other times, the last sentence acts as a bridge (or transition) to the next paragraph. Finally, when you start a new paragraph you always indent the first line (you move it in a few spaces).

Take a look at this paragraph from one of our workshops. We have marked the sentences so that you can tell which is the topic sentence, which are detail sentences, and which is the wrap-up.

### A Special Day in the Park

Every year, my family celebrates "Ramos Day" in a park in our neighborhood. All the relatives come, even from as far away as Texas. Everyone from my grandmother to the newest grandchild is there. My sister makes a banner and hangs it between two big trees. My sisters and I sing in harmony and my brothers play guitar. The children play games and the adults play cards. There is lots of good food because everyone cooks and brings their special dish. It is a wonderful day and a tradition that we will continue.

Keeping this paragraph in mind, try to write one of your own.

---

### Writing Exercise

For five minutes, write about one thing, person, or incident that you saw on the way to class today. You can start the first sentence with, "On the way to class I saw . . ."

### Reflections

Look back at the first sentence of the piece you just wrote. It should be the most general. Are there any ideas or sentences that do not relate directly to that sentence? If there are, take them out. In general, paragraphs need one central idea, which is supported by detail sentences that tell you more about the central idea.

---

### Paragraph Practice

Try writing a paragraph from our map. (See Figure 2.)

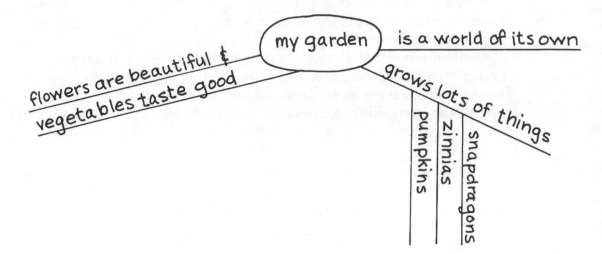

Figure 2. Garden Map

Your paragraph should read roughly like this:

My garden is a wonderful place. It is a world of its own. I grow a lot of different things, including snapdragons, zinnias, and huge pumpkins. The flowers are beautiful and the vegetables taste good.

Another important thing about paragraphs is that they should make sense. They need to have an organizational pattern in which one idea follows another. When one idea is out of whack, it throws off the whole paragraph.

This next exercise is all about organization. We took a simple paragraph about changing a tire and mixed it up so you could see what having things out of order could do.

## Practice Writing Organized

This paragraph is an organizational nightmare, rewrite it so that it makes sense. After you have finished, check your paragraph with ours.

On the way to class this morning, my car got a flat tire. With my new tire in place, I sped along to school. I couldn't quite remember how to change a tire but a passing driver stopped to help. We took the old tire off and put it in the trunk. The jack was hard to work but we finally managed. The old tire was hard to get off because the lugs were rusted. The new tire went on in no time.

Here is our paragraph.

On the way to class this morning, my car got a flat tire. I couldn't quite remember how to change a tire but a passing driver stopped to help. The jack was difficult to use but we finally managed. The old tire was hard to get off because the lugs were rusty. We took the old tire off and put it in the trunk. The new tire went on in no time. With my new tire in place, I sped along to school.

---

## Writing Exercise

Write a mixed-up paragraph giving directions or retelling an event in which sequence is important. Find a partner and trade paragraphs to unravel.

---

### *Journal Entry:*

Write a paragraph about a routine that you do every day, such as fixing breakfast or getting to work.

OR

Write about a family tradition.

# Unit II

# Telling Stories:
# Personal Narrative

You are stranded in a country store in the middle of a small town in Vermont. There is a terrible blizzard, it's cold, and there is no such thing as a motel. Six other people are sitting around the pot-bellied stove, drinking coffee, and talking. Even the owner of the store can't go home because the roads are too slick. He agrees to keep making coffee and let everyone stay there until the weather lets up. To pass the time, people begin to tell stories. One man talks about the day his heifer got loose and went into the church. Another woman talks about the day her son glued his brother's plate to the table. Finally it comes around to you. What story from your life would you tell?

---

### Writing Exercise

Write for ten minutes about a story from your own life.

### Reflections

Think for a minute about what it was like to write your story. Now, respond to these questions:

What are the kinds of images and ideas that went through your head?
What kinds of events did you think about?
Did you think about what people or objects looked like?
What kinds of sounds did you hear?

---

All of those things are part of narrative writing. Simply put, narratives are stories. It's as easy as telling about the soaps, passing time in a storm, or talking about yourself and your home town. Narratives are used every day when you answer the question "What happened?" or "What did you do?" It is the most like storytelling of all the kinds of writing.

*WRITE 5 minutes*

*9/06*

---

## Writing Exercise

Turn to someone, even your pet or your plant, and tell him or her how your day has been so far. Try to talk for at least one full minute. (The average person speaks about 150 words per minute.)

Now, write down how your day has been. Try to write for five minutes. Include as many of the details of your day that you just described to your plant, pet, or partner.

## Reflections

*9/06*

Count up the number of words you wrote. How close were you to 150? A common length for lots of writing assignments is 150 words. We think it's a good idea to start thinking about what 150 words really means. (Though it is too early to worry much about length.) Write down some of the differences you found between writing and speaking about your day. Remember, if you can say it, you can write it.

---

Writing is one of the best ways to describe how you are feeling, and writing personal narratives is one of the most fun ways to describe your thoughts. It's up to you to decide whether or not to share your work with someone else, but we do suggest that you read your work out loud as often as possible.

## STORIES ABOUT YOU

As we have said, the best way to learn how to write better is to write about something you know a lot about. Most people would agree that the one topic where they are experts is themselves. In the next few pages we will focus on stories from your own life.

## Writing Exercise

There are two versions of this same exercise. You can choose to do both of them or only one. This is best done with a partner or in groups of three or four but can be done alone.

*Scar Stories 1.* Most people have at least one scar some place on their bodies. How that scar came to be is the source of a good story. Find a scar you are particularly fond of and write down how you got it. If you don't have any physical scars at all, not even a tiny one left over from a skinned knee, then make up a story about how you would like to have gotten a scar. It can be as dramatic and silly as you want. Read/share the scar stories with the group or with one other person.

*Scar Stories 2.* On a sheet of paper write only the beginning of how you got your favorite scar. Make sure you set the stage and include the necessary pieces of the tale but don't finish the story! Trade papers with your partner or someone in your group and let him or her finish the story. Compare notes to see how close or far off you both were in ending the story.

## Reflections

What were the details included in the beginning of the story that lead you to write your conclusion?
What did you like best about the story?
Share your scar stories with other people in your class.

## Writing Exercise

Write another story about your life. This time pick an event that made you laugh. As you do this exercise work through these steps (the five-step writing process from Unit 1):

*Step 1: Brainstorm*   Write down three events that made you laugh, and select one of them to write about. Circle it.

*Step 2: List*   Make a list of as many details about the incident as you can remember. Try to include people, places, sounds, the weather, time of day, etc. Practice writing in complete sentences.

*Step 3: Write*   Arrange those sentences and add more to make a first draft of your story.

*Step 4: Edit*  Read your story out loud to another person in the class. Ask them to answer these questions for you.

1. What did you like best about the story?
2. What would you like to know more about?
3. Does the story move logically from the beginning to the end? Are there any pieces that seem out of order, if so what are they?

*Step 5: Rewrite*  Now, paying attention to these comments, rewrite your story as a final draft. Notice your paragraphs, in particular. Your story might have a few main ideas. This would mean that you would have more than one paragraph.

## Writing Exercise

As you know, everyone has stories. Everyone has at least one unusual event in her or his life. Pick one out of your life and write about it for ten minutes. It could be an event from your childhood, something unusual that happened at work, or something special that your family has done.

## Reflections

Read what you have just written out loud to someone else. How does your story sound? Are there any places where you run out of breath when reading a sentence or a place where the sentences seem choppy? The problem could be in the punctuation. To help you make your writing sound better, we are going to spend some time on punctuation.

## Punctuation Pointers: Capitals, Periods, and Complete Thoughts

All sentences should start with capital letters.
All sentences should end with an end mark (period, question mark, exclamation point).
All sentences should be one complete thought.

Take the breath test. Read your story out loud again and look at the length of the sentences. As a general rule of thumb, if you run out of breath trying to read it, the sentence is too long. You can divide the long sentence into two short sentences by putting a period where your voice naturally stops. Make sure you begin the next sentence with a capital letter.

## Punctuation Practice

Let's polish these few sentences from a true story by a woman in our class. We changed it around a little to practice punctuation. Read the story out loud to yourself.

### The Day They Switched My Baby

I'll never forget the time they switched my baby that was crazy I was the only black woman in the hospital and they brought me the wrong baby the baby they brought me was a girl my baby was a boy

By the time that you get to the end of the story you should be out of breath. This is because there is no punctuation in it. Periods tell the reader when to stop and when to breathe.

Write the story over again and add the periods where you think they should go (except for the title—titles do not have periods). Remember: Every time you start a new sentence, you have to capitalize the beginning letter. When you have finished rewriting the story, check your punctuation with ours, as follows:

### The Day They Switched My Baby

I'll never forget the time they switched my baby. That was crazy. I was the only black woman in the hospital and they brought me the wrong baby. The baby they brought me was a white girl. My baby was a boy.

## Yet Another Punctuation Exercise

Go back to the story you wrote about your unusual event. Go through the same steps you just did in the "baby" example. If needed, write a corrected version. Read it out loud to yourself or someone else. How does it sound? If you are still feeling unsure about capitals and periods, do the next exercise.

## Even More Punctuation Practice

This is another, longer story from our writing class. We have taken out most of the periods and capital letters. Put the periods and capitals back in the story. When you are finished, check your story with ours (which is at the end of the unit).

*Practice 1.*

I lived in a field near a town in Puerto Rico at this date, I did not have a washing machine and had to wash the clothes in the ravine or in the river we had to lay them to dry on the grates of the wire fence. This time I dried my clothes like I always did but with bad luck there were bulls fenced in the field. when I returned for my dry clothes I found them scattered in the field some of the bulls had my clothes on their horns. Tears came to my eyes because I had lost my clothes later I laughed to see the bulls running in the field with clothes between their horns resembling small flags.

Now that you have done the breath test to get a feel for where punctuation goes, let's try a slightly harder way to recognize complete sentences.

We have found in our workshops that folks often have trouble with the idea that a sentence needs to be one complete thought. In its simplest form a sentence is a finished idea. For example, look at these two "sentences." One is a complete thought or finished idea and one is not.

1. John Jones plays a fine blues guitar.
2. John Jones, the man with the gold tooth.

You probably figured out that Sentence 1 is a complete thought or finished idea. From the sentence, you know that John Jones (subject) plays (the verb or action word) a fine blues guitar (the object). In Sentence 2 the idea is not finished. You are left hanging. You know that John Jones is still the subject. You know a little about him (he has a gold tooth). But John Jones does not do anything, the verb is missing. The idea is not finished. For practice, try the next exercise.

## Complete Idea Exercise

Some of the phrases below are incomplete sentences. Just to be sneaky, we have put periods at the end of all of the phrases and capitals at the beginning of all the phrases. Some of the phrases need a beginning; some need an end. Some are just fine. Pick out the incomplete sentences. For fun, make them complete or finished ideas. You can be as creative as you want. Our answers are at the end of the unit.

1. Redd Fox was a famous comedian.
2. The Cincinnati Reds, a great ball team.
3. My Dad was born in Jamaica.
4. Salmon are tasty fish.
5. Fishing for salmon is.
6. Who is a wonderful person.
7. Runs on a mixture of gas and oil.
8. Singing makes folks happy.

9. Beans and rice are.
10. Singing the blues on the bayou.

## Yet Another Complete Idea Exercise

Incomplete sentences are harder to find when they are not by themselves. This is because when folks read they sometimes make corrections in their heads that are not on the paper. A good way around this problem is to read what you wrote in reverse order. In other words, read the last sentence first, then the next to last sentence, and so on. You need to look at each sentence on its own.

A paragraph follows that has some incomplete sentences (ideas). See how many you can find. Our answers are at the end of the unit.

### The Blues

Much of today's music has its roots in the blues. Blues music started in the American south. In the early part of this century. The blues grew out of many sources. Such as music and lyrics from African-American spirituals and rural folk songs.

The irony of the blues is that it uses sad stories to cheer people up. Many rock musicians use the blues music style in their own writing. The haunting minor chords and the sad lyrics can be found in everything. From Chuck Berry to Led Zeppelin.

## LETTER WRITING AS STORY TELLING

Letters have always been a way for people to keep in touch with each other. This was especially true before the days of the telephone. For most of us, there is still something very special about going to the mailbox and finding a letter from a friend. Letters are also a perfect way to practice narrative writing.

---

### Writing Exercise

Write a letter to a member of your family who is far away, telling him or her about something special or different that you have done recently. It may be as straightforward as going to a movie or returning to school to get your GED. It could be an incident from church or an event from your neighborhood. Write the letter exactly as if you were going to send it.

We are going to use this letter writing exercise to work on another useful punctuation tool, which is the comma.

## Punctuation Pointers: Commas

Commas are one of the most useful punctuation marks around. As a rule of thumb, commas occur inside a sentence when your voice drops or you pause. *Example:* Read this sentence out loud:

Marlene the lady with the blond hair is sitting in the front row.

Now read the same sentence and pause when you get to the commas.

Marlene, the lady with the blond hair, is sitting in the front row.

The second sentence should make more sense and sound better to you. That is because it has commas.

Commas have many uses and are covered by many rules. We have chosen a few rules to share with you that our students have found to be the most useful.

Five common uses of commas are:

1.  To separate items in a series.
    *Example:* a dog, a cat, and an elephant.
2.  To set off descriptive phrases in a sentence.
    *Example:* Eileen's house, the large brick one, is on the corner.
    We call this rule the "detail door." A comma opens the door, lets the detail in, then a comma closes the door.
3.  To separate two independent clauses. Independent clauses are like two little sentences joined together. The sentences are put together by joining words or *conjunctions.* The conjunctions are: *and, but, for, or, so, yet, nor.* The comma comes *before* the joining word. (This is easier than it sounds.)
    *Examples:* John is getting his GED, and he hopes to go to college. Betty is working at night now, but she hopes to move to the day shift soon.
4.  To set off dates: May 25, 1991.
    To set off places: Geneva, New York
5.  Commas are used at the beginning and ending of letters such as: Dear Mary,/Love, John

## Comma Practice

Return to the letter you just wrote. Read each sentence out loud and add commas where you think they belong. If possible, trade letters with a partner and see if you both agree on your use of commas.

## More Comma Practice

Below are excerpts from a real Civil War letter that was found in Bird's attic. The man, George Browne, is writing home to his mother in Rhode Island. Correct each of the sentences using commas, periods, and capital letters. Compare your answers to ours at the end of the unit.

*Practice 2.*

July 1 1863

Mother

(1) Your letter written May 25 just came to hand today.

(2) I don't recollect where I was when I last wrote you but I think it was lancaster kentucky

(3) from there we went to crab orchard somerset and back to lancaster

(4) these marches are about 60 miles on foot the soldiers are carrying very heavy loads and the weather is very war.

(5) we are now near the cumberland river a place that is a lot cooler than our last camp and we have shower baths wood and plenty of water.

(6) my troops anxious to go home are singing very lively in this beautiful grove overlooking the village

(7) I had a letter from sam and he said that john is away to the west I am sorry that I could not see him before he left I hope and pray to be home soon

respectfully

your son george browne

*Journal Entry:* Choose one topic.

Write a story from your own childhood that you would want passed along to another generation.

OR

Write about a time in your life when you felt most relieved.

# DESCRIPTIVE WRITING

You are talking on the phone with an old friend from your school days, whom you haven't seen in years. The friend has moved away and is thinking about making a trip back home, but she wants to know what to expect. She asks you to describe what you see out the window as you are talking on the phone. How would you answer your friend?

---

### Writing Exercise

Freewrite for ten minutes about what you see out your window at home. Close your eyes and get a picture in your mind before you start writing.

### Reflections

Respond to these questions:
Were you successful in visualizing the scene from your window?
What sounds, smells, and textures did you include?
What image did you focus on and why?
How would you describe this same scene to a person who was sight or hearing impaired?

---

What you have just done is a quick example of descriptive writing. In a nutshell, descriptive writing is like being a photographer or a painter. Instead of film or paint, a writer uses words to create an image for the reader. A photographer can capture the beauty of a sunrise on a beach by framing the scene, setting the light meter, and clicking the shutter. A writer, however, must use words to convey the sound of the surf, the light on the beach, and the cry of the gulls to create the same image.

---

### Writing Exercise

Shut your eyes and think about an object, picture it in your mind. Write about that object for a few minutes without ever saying exactly what the object is. Read your description to a partner. Can she or he figure out what you are writing about? Why or why not?

---

## Adjectives: The Key to Descriptive Writing

A key to descriptive writing is the use of adjectives. These are words that give the characteristics of a person, place, or thing. For example, *luscious, skinny, delicate, strong,* and *fuzzy* are adjectives. The best way to practice descriptive writing is to practice thinking of and using adjectives.

## Writing Exercise

Find a partner and then select as many of the following items as you wish. For each one, you and your partner list as many words as you can think of that describe the characteristics of the item. For example, some possible adjectives for *taxicab: yellow, rusty, checkered, dented, dirty, clean, speedy, clunky, smelly,* and so on!

| | | | |
|---|---|---|---|
| a taxicab | your birthday | a city lit up | an apple |
| a popsicle | your shoes | at night | pie |
| your bedroom | your hand | chocolate | a thunder- |
| a beach | shrimp | a cow | storm |
| severe | a meadow in | a sidewalk | a traffic jam |
| temperature | summer | after the rain | an eye |
| a victory/loss | | a palm tree | the moon |

*(handwritten: 10/06)*
*(handwritten: 100°)*

Using the list you've just generated, write sentences describing the object. It is helpful to pretend that you're communicating with someone who has no idea what you are describing. If you can, read your sentences to others in the class and get their feedback.

Another way of thinking about descriptive writing is that it communicates the textures, sounds, tastes, and smells of life to readers. Descriptive writing makes your work richer and more interesting to read. Description can also communicate emotions such as fear, love, excitement, and joy as well as convey urgency, anger, and heartache. Simple statements such as "I am angry" are made more interesting by including the characteristics of the emotion.

## Writing Exercise

Add to these simple statements to make a more complete description. Try to make the image as vivid as possible. Share with a partner. *For example:*

I was nervous. My palms began to sweat and my stomach hurt. I could feel my face getting hot, and my throat was so dry I could barely talk.

I was nervous.  *afraid*
Jake was excited.

My friend was devastated.
Mother was furious.
The ocean was calm.
Alan is handsome.
The scenery was spectacular.
The lake's beauty stunned me.
Clearly, the child was terrified.
Football is very intense.
The soldier looked so lonely.
Gwen is awesome.

## Metaphors and Similes

Another important tool in descriptive writing is the use of figures of speech such as similes and metaphors. A *simile* is a comparison using "like" or "as." For example, from the theme song from the movie *The Rose* there is a line that goes "I say love is like a flower and you its only seed." Obviously love is not a plant, it is an emotion. The simile works because the image of love growing into a beautiful flower is reasonable.

A *metaphor* is a figure of speech in which a word or phrase suggests a comparison or an identity. Metaphors are a compact and colorful way of expressing complex and elaborate ideas. For example, Bette Midler in the movie *The Rose* refers to being a "waitress at the banquet of life." What that means is that life was passing her by. The phrase "she is a tigress" implies all sorts of ideas and emotions from anger to passion without actually writing it all out.

Metaphors and similes can make your writing more vivid and more powerful. Song writers, essayists, and novelists all use metaphors and similes.

### Writing Exercise

Below are a series of metaphors and similes from popular songs and stories. Read each one and indicate if the phrase is a metaphor or simile and then write what you think it means in the same way as we did in the example from *The Rose*. Check your answers with ours.

*Practice 3.*

1. "I am a rock, I am an island. . . . A rock feels no pain, and an island never cries."

   —*Simon and Garfunkle*

2. "She's like the wind in my trees."

*—Patrick Swazyee*

3. "You are the dreamer's only dream."

*—Bee Gees*

4. "She's like a cool summer breeze."

*—Little Feet*

5. "Oh love is handsome, love is fine. Love is a jewel when it is new . . ."

*—Traditional folk song*

6. "Goodnight you moonlight ladies . . ."

*—James Taylor*

7. "She is as cold as the soles of a gravedigger's feet . . ."

*—Traditional*

8. "He is meaner than a snake and colder than charity . . ."

*—Traditional*

9. "I'm a crawling king snake and I rule my den."

*—John Lee Hooker*

Now that you have had a chance to work with other people's metaphors and similes, try to write some of your own. Remember similes use "like" or "as" and metaphors do not. Do the following exercise alone or with a partner.

## Writing Exercise

Select at least four of these items and write a metaphor or simile for each one. Share these with other people in your class or try them out on a friend.

1. Any member of your family
2. Your best friend
3. A car you have always wanted
4. A garden
5. Your house or apartment
6. A duck
7. A sunrise or sunset
8. A roller coaster ride
9. Fishing in a pond in the summer
10. A peppermint patty

*Journal Entry:* Choose one topic.
Describe a place that you really like.
OR
Describe an event from your life when you were very afraid.

## Descriptive Writing:
## Fantasy Versus Fact

Up until now, the writing we have been doing has been generally factual—that is about people, things, places that you know and that probably exist. Of course, another kind of descriptive writing is when you write fiction. It's like daydreaming. This kind of writing is important because you learn to relax and concentrate on using as much imagery as you can. As a result, your other writing gets better.

---

### Writing Exercise

Freewrite for ten minutes about winning the lottery.

### Reflections

Respond to these questions:

What happened when you wrote about winning the lottery?
How was this writing different from your other writing?

---

### Writing Exercise

Choose a trip that you have always wanted to take and haven't because of time or money. Describe the trip in as much detail as you can. What would you do? Where would you stay? What would you see?

---

## Editing Practice:
## Content and Punctuation

Trade trip descriptions with a partner and practice editing each others. Do it in two steps—first content, and second punctuation. If you do not have a partner, answer these questions by yourself.

## Content Questions:

1. What did you like best about the description?
2. What would you like to know more about?
3. What metaphors or similes were used? If none, try to suggest some.

## Punctuation Questions:

1. Do all the sentences start with capitals?
2. Are there periods at the end of each sentence?
3. Are there any sentences that should be two sentences instead of one?
4. Are the commas in the right place? (Remember the detail door.)

Rewrite your trip description in a final draft.

---

### Writing Exercise

One of the interesting things about looking at old photos is wondering about the people and the places in them. Each one tells a story and each one is a great chance to practice your writing. Choose one of the two versions of this exercise:

*A:* Find an old photo of an unfamiliar family member or place and write a descriptive story about the picture.

*B:* If you are in a class, bring in a photo from your collection and trade with a partner. Write a descriptive story about your partner's picture. Trade stories. Edit using the questions from the previous exercise.

---

*Journal Entry:*

Describe your "dream home."

OR

Describe your "ideal" partner.

Now that we have spent some time describing people and places we will move on to writing about those people and places from different points of view.

# POINT OF VIEW

Ever wondered what it would be like to be somebody other than yourself? Ever watch television and think about being your favorite character? Have you ever seen a movie where the people trade places, such as the mother becomes the daughter, or a person turns into an animal like a dog?

---

**\*\*Freewrite for five minutes.\*\***

Choose someone that you would like to trade places with and write what your life would be like.

## Reflections

What changed about the way you thought as you were writing?

---

The writing skill that you have just experimented with is called *point of view*. Point of view is simply writing from different perspectives.

## Foolish Fairy Tales Writing Exercise

There are two versions of this exercise; choose one. (It's more fun if you work in groups).

*A:* Pick one of the these old favorite children's tales and do a quick retelling; share your story with the group:

"Three Blind Mice" from the point of view of the farmer's wife
"Little Red Riding Hood" from the point of view of the wolf
"Three Little Pigs" from the point of view of the wolf
"Snow White and the Seven Dwarfs" from the point of view of the stepmother

*B:* Choose any favorite story and do a quick retelling from the point of view of another character. If possible, share your stories with the class.

---

## Reflections

As you took on the point of view of another character how did your writing change?

---

---

### Writing Exercise

This is another way of practicing writing from different points of view. Pick an event from your own life and write about it twice. Choose one of the pairs of different points of view:

You as a child; you as an adult
Two onlookers, one old and one young
You and one of your parents
A person who knows you well and a total stranger

### Reflections

Compare your pieces. How are they the same? How are they different?
How did the way you organized your piece change?
What generalizations can you make so far about writing from different points of view?

---

## Tone or Voice

*Tone* or *voice* is the way a story sounds. For example, people shouting at each other gives a very different impression than people whispering. When people are happy they sound and choose words that are different from when they a.. angry. Tom Liner and Dan Kirby (1981) describe three kinds of these voices or tones as "mad talking," "soft talking," and "fast talking." We added "happy talking" because we're such sentimentalists.

*Mad talking* is the voice you use when you are angry.
*Happy talking* is the voice you use when your are content or glad.
*Soft talking* is the voice you use when you want to make someone sad feel better.
*Fast talking* is used when you are in a tight spot and need to do some fancy footwork to get yourself out.

---

### Writing Exercise—Voices

In this exercise we are going to do a series of quick freewrites to practice using these voices. Write only for five minutes in each of these voices. Choose only one from the list of ideas for each voice.

### Mad talking

Write about a time when you were very angry.
Write about a time when something you loved got broken by someone else.
Write what you would say if someone stole something from you that you loved, including your husband, wife, girlfriend, or boyfriend.

### Happy Talking

Write about a time when you were very happy.
Write about how you would feel if you fulfilled a long awaited dream.
Write about your favorite moment from childhood.

### Soft Talking

Comfort a lost child.
Calm a frightened animal.
Calm a frantic parent.

### Fast talking

Write about a young person explaining a bad report card.
Write about explaining to "your" boyfriend or girlfriend why you have a book of matches from a fancy restaurant where he or she has never been.
Write about getting out of the tight spot of your choice.

## Reflections

This exercise is more fun when you can do it with at least three other people, but it can be done alone. Make a chart that looks like Figure 3.

In your small group look back over your three pieces, sort out the similarities you find in each of the kinds of writing and put them on your chart (see our example). Look for general things, such as length of sentences, kinds of words used, and types of topics.

Look back at your chart and answer these questions:

| mad | short words with lots of short vowels | short sentences | "stinky topics" |
|------|------|------|------|
| happy | | | |
| soft | | | |
| fast | | | |

Figure 3.   Comparing Voices

How are all your pieces the same?
How are they different?
Which piece was the hardest to write?
Which piece was the easiest?
Why do you think that is so?

Compare charts with other people in your class.

## Point of View in Stories

Stories need a teller. That means that stories are written or told from different points of view. A fancy word for point of view is narration. The storyteller is often called the narrator. There are lots of different points of view or ways to narrate a story. In fact, whole books have been written about narration in literature. For our purposes though, we really need to be concerned with only a few of them.

1.   One very common point of view is the *first-person narrative*. The teller uses lots of I, Me, My, We, Us, Our. For example, the movie *Out of Africa* starts with, "I had a farm in Africa. I had a farm in Africa at the foot of the Ngong hills." The story is told from the point of view of the main character, and it is about her life. What we hear is *her* perspective and thoughts.

Here is another example of first-person narrative. Notice the use of the word *we*. The story is being told from the point of view of a group.

She was a permanent fixture in our town, as permanent as the church and the general store but not as good or as useful as either one. We would always see her walking down the street, dressed in black, with an ostrich feather in her hat. As the years rolled by, she grew older and smaller, as if she were determined to simply shrink into the earth rather than depart from it.

2. Another common way to tell a story is called *third-person narrative.* The teller uses lots of He, She, His, Her, They. Third-person narrative comes in two types: limited and objective. Stories written in third-person objective are like a newspaper article or a fairy tale. The narrator is outside the story and relates what happens without any comments. You do not know what the characters are thinking, only what they are doing. Stories may begin "once upon a time, when all the world was young," and spin on from there.

   In third-person limited, the story is told from one character's viewpoint. The story shows one person's thoughts, feelings, and actions. *For example:*

   > Quickly darting away from the car, ace detective John Stone drew his weapon. Just as he was about to fire, a brutal explosion flung him back. "This can only mean one thing," he thought, "Dr. Moon has returned."

3. A third common way to tell a story is as if you were a mind reader for all the characters. (The fancy way of saying this is *third-person omniscient,* which means "all-knowing.") Just as in third-person narrative, the teller still reports on the actions of the characters. The difference is that in third-person omniscient, the teller knows all the characters' thoughts and memories. The reader has no sense of the teller. *For Example:*

   > The plains stretched out endlessly in front of the wagons, and the sun beat down without mercy. The two children rocked gently on the wagon seat as the oxen plowed across the prairie. The youngest child, Lisa, was totally lost in thought. "I wonder if I will like my new home, I wonder if we will live on a farm." Her sister, Anne, also began to think. She thought about her old bedroom at the top of the stairs and began to miss it very much. "Will I find friends?" she pondered. Both children were worried about what life held in store for them.

## Practice Exercise

This exercise is mostly for people who are around young children and who like to listen to stories (who doesn't?). Find four children's stories that you might like to read. Study the way the authors use point of view.

## Writing Exercise

Write a story for a child. This will give you a chance to practice some of the skills you have worked with up to now. Just to get you going, we will give you some characters you might use in your story: an old one-eyed man, a magical fish, and an orphan. Pick a point of view (even your own) and have a good time. When you are finished, read it to a child.

*Journal Entry:*

Daydream yourself as a famous athlete. Write about your most spectacular game. You may want to write it from the point of view of the TV sportscaster.

OR

Describe yourself to yourself. When you are finished, describe yourself from the point of view of someone else.

## COLLECTING INFORMATION

In this next section we are going to think about and do a writing project using family histories. When you work through a longer piece of writing like this, you get a chance to practice writing, sorting, and collecting information from others. The biggest part of collecting information is learning how to ask questions to get the information you want.

Learning to write good questions is important because it helps you to think clearly and precisely about what you are writing (reporters do it all the time). Questions are like hooks on which you can hang information. General questions will get you big pieces of information. Specific questions will give you important details. Working this way gives your writing a skeleton. Let's try it.

## Writing Exercise

Freewrite for ten minutes, as if you were talking to a stranger, about where you grew up. Tell how your family came to live there and describe the place.

### Reflections

1.  Look over the piece you have just written and make a list of the most important GENERAL points.

2. Make up questions that ask for the same kind of information you have just chosen as your most important points.

3. In order to check to see if the questions you wrote would get the information you want, reread the piece you just wrote. Are the answers to the questions in the piece? Is there something missing? Is there something you would like to know more about? If you answered "yes" to any of the above, write some more questions.

## Practice Exercise

Here is a piece of family history from Bird's family. This is a true story. What you will read is a very brief version of a much longer piece. Read it and write a series of general and specific questions that you would ask that would help you to rewrite this piece to be more interesting. (Pretend for a minute that you are a reporter covering a story).

On your paper, mark which questions are general and which are specific. Compare your questions with ours. What are the similarities and what are the differences?

OPTIONAL: Rewrite the story; feel free to make up any information you want.

### Kidnapped

My great-great-great grandfather Mario came to this country by accident. When he was only eleven he and his friend Phillipe were playing in a rowboat just off a beach in Sardinia. A British warship came in and kidnapped the boys. They were forced to work on the ship. Life was hard and Phillipe died. One day the ship sailed into New London harbor in what is now Connecticut. The sailors came ashore with Mario. As soon as his feet touched dry land he began to run to freedom. He ran into a field of farmers hoeing their crops. The farmers went after the sailors with their hoes and chased them away. Mario was adopted by a farm family, learned English, and eventually grew up. He married, had many children, and lived to be an old man.

### Our Questions:

1. What did the boys look like?
2. Where is Sardinia and what does it look like?
3. What about their family?
4. What did they do exactly on the boat?
5. What happened when the sailors chased him?
6. What happened to him in America?
7. Did he ever go back to Sardinia? If so, what did he find?

## Interviewing

*Interviewing* is the art of asking questions of others.

Now that you have practiced writing questions, find a partner and do this exercise together.

1.  *Write* a series of questions as if you were a newspaper reporter snooping out the history of your partner's family.
2.  *Interview* your partner and jot down the answers to the questions.
3.  *Sort* the information. Think about what would go in which paragraphs. Use your mapping skills.
4.  *Write* the story.
5.  *Read* it out loud to your partner and *edit* it together.

Now that you have had a chance to practice interviewing others, we are going to turn to practicing dialogue. Dialogue is a useful writing tool because it adds more interest to your writing and lets you branch out into more complex pieces.

## Dialogue

Bird's Dad always starts a story by lighting his pipe, settling into his chair and saying "Once upon a time, when all the world was young" or "That reminds me of the time . . ." The tale spins on from there. Every time a new character comes on the scene, his voice changes to sound like the speaker. As you know, those voices and conversations are called *dialogue.*

Unfortunately, there are many grammar rules for writing dialogue. We have selected some of the most useful rules for you.

To further help you out with writing dialogue, we wrote a few paragraphs of dialogue so you can copy the *way* that the dialogue is set up. So, when you are in doubt about how to use punctuation in dialogue, just check the example at the end of the rules.

**Some basics on dialogue:**

Don't try to learn these all at once, but use this as a resource.

1.  Quotation marks are used to mark dialogue or quotes. Quotation marks look like this: "                  "
2.  Punctuation marks almost always go inside quotation marks: "I love this town."
3.  Question marks and exclamation points are almost always at the end of the quotation (inside the quotation marks). For example:

    "Run!" or "Is it going to rain today?" he asked.

4.  For a piece of dialogue or a quotation that ends in a period, the period always goes at the end of the *sentence* (even if the quotation is only part of the sentence!). For example:

> "John is going to the store," he said.
> She thought, "Boy, it is getting late."

5.  When you are writing dialogue and the quote is not at the end of the sentence, you need to put a comma when the person stops talking. For example:

> "John is going to the store," he said.

6.  Each time someone new speaks, you change paragraphs. In dialogue this means you start a new line. Example:

> "That is a beautiful dress, did you buy it here?"
> "No, I made it."
> "Wow! That is wonderful."

7.  When one person speaks a bunch of sentences in a row, you put quotation marks around the first word of the first sentence and the last word of the last sentence. For example:

> "It was October 4th, 1947 when I first saw the UFOs. I was out walking my dog. It was a night more cloudy than an English winter and more windy than a Chicago afternoon. That's when I saw them."

*Note:* This rule is only true if you don't ever put in descriptions on how someone said something. If you do it looks like this:

> "I like milk," she declared. "It tastes great."

Or even like this:

> "Turn left by that big oak," he explained, "and right by the brook."

8.  Last but not least, and this is a tough one, we need to discuss capitalization in dialogue. First, you need to capitalize the first word at the beginning of a quotation, even if it is in the middle of the sentence. For example:

> Regina ran out in the middle of the road and screamed, "Come back you scoundrel! Come Back!"

Second, when your sentence finishes with a phrase such as "he said," you <u>do not</u> capitalize the *he/she/they/them*. For example:

> "Mother Earth is our friend, Johnny; but we must learn to respect her," she said.

Here is that model of dialogue we promised. It contains examples of all of the previous rules. Use it as a reference.

He looked at her with the type of stare that would stop the sun. "Sit down," he demanded. Lily, only two years old (but ten years old in dog years), sat.

"What did I do now?" the young puppy thought. "Was it the five pairs of sneakers that I ate? Perhaps it was the cushion of the brand new couch? Or even the extended-wear contact lenses that I stole off the bathroom sink."

"How many times have I told you not to go into my room?" he asked sharply. "Are you deaf? Don't I feed you and take you for walks?"

Lily thought to herself, "Who takes who for walks?"

"What do you have to say for yourself?" he demanded.

"Woof."

"Woof? Woof is all you have to say?" he sighed. "What am I going to do," he moaned, "with a weed whacker on four legs?"

*Practice 4.*

# Dialogue Practice

Below is a story with lots of dialogue. Rewrite the story putting in the quotation marks and making the right words capitalized. Remember to make new paragraphs every time a new person speaks. Our corrected version is at the back of the unit. *Note:* This is the beginning of an unfinished children's story. Feel free to finish it, or if you have children, finish it with them.

(1) Bertha Snoot sat on her couch, blowing huge pink strawberry gum bubbles. (2) My life is so boring, she said to herself. (3) Nothing ever happens to me. (4) All I do is sit around.

(5) Suddenly Bertha Snoot heard a knock on her door. (6) She peeped through the spy hole and to her surprise, there stood a very elegant redheaded woman dressed in purple satin. (7) May I come in? she asked. (8) I am not from the Department of Health, the Urban League, or the United Way. (9) I don't sell vacuum cleaners or magazines, or give away soap. (10) Her voice was as soft and silky as the whiskers on Bertha Snoot's cat, Bombay. (11) If you don't sell anything and aren't from anywhere, who are you? inquired Miss Snoot. (12) Why, isn't it obvious? said the strange woman. (13) I am your travel agent, your ticket to adventure and romance. (14) Just let me in, she cooed. (15) A few moments of your time is all I ask. (16) Bertha Snoot was indeed intrigued. (17) What a boring life, what a boring apartment, what could it hurt? (18) I could just listen for a minute, she whispered to herself. (19) I'll just let her in for a minute.

(20) With that Bertha Snoot opened her apartment door. (21) Little did she know that her life and her cat's would never be the same again.

---

### Writing Exercise

Now that you have had a chance to practice using dialogue, try to write some of your own. Choose one of the two versions of this exercise.

*A.* Write for ten minutes about a conversation you would love to have with someone famous. What would you talk about? What would he/she say? It can be as outlandish as you want.

*B.* Listen in on a real conversation and try to write it down as carefully as you can. Bring it back to class. Don't tell anyone anything about the people or the situation. Share your "conversation" with a partner or with a group and ask them to fill in as much detail as they can, using only what you have given them as clues. For example, who do they think is talking? What do they think is the setting?

---

## SUMMARY WRITING: SHORT AND SWEET

Learning to write only the bare bones of an idea is an important skill. The next few exercises will help you practice cutting your writing down to size.

Pretend you are about to make a long distance call to someone dear to you and very far away. The call will cost $23,000 for five minutes. (No, you can't opt to keep the money.) You won't be talking to this person again for ten years. What would you say?

---

**Freewrite for five minutes on the $23,000 phone call.**

### Reflections

1. What happened when you began to think about talking for five minutes at such expense?
2. Did you just start chatting away or did you think about how to organize your thoughts?
3. How did you decide what was important and what wasn't?

---

What you have just done is a summary. When you summarize something you include only the most important ideas. You try to tell someone something using the least number of words possible. At the same time, you want your ideas to be crystal clear and to the point. In summary writing there isn't any room for "fluff." As Sergeant Friday used to say on the old television show *Dragnet*, "Give me the facts ma'am—just the facts."

---

### Writing Exercise

Choose one of these exercises.

*A:* Find a lead article in a newspaper and write a one-paragraph summary about what it said.

*B:* Find a partner who watches the same soap opera that you watch. Agree to watch one show at the same time. Write a one-paragraph summary about what you saw. Compare paragraphs. They should be about the same. If not, work together to rewrite the summary.

---

*Journal entry:*
   Summarize your day.

## GRAMMAR GREMLINS: PARALLEL CONSTRUCTION

We are going to take a short break from writing paragraphs and stories to focus on one of the demons of grammar. We call them "grammar gremlins" because they can be so ornery and cause so much mischief in your writing. One particular trouble spot for folks is a beast called *parallel construction* (it's popular on the GED exam).

Parallel construction is a fancy way of saying, "Keep things the same." When you use parallel structure in a sentence, you repeat similar words or phrases to show similar ideas. Think of it this way: Sentence construction is like doing the laundry; you shouldn't mix your whites and your colors or you can get a mess. Let's do some examples:

You wouldn't say, "The things I like most are eating, worked, and running." The word *worked* is out of place—it should be *working*, just like the rest.

Here is another example:

Bertha Snoot loves soap operas that are sappy and that are boring.

The phrases "that are sappy" and "that are boring" are similar because they both use the word *that.* They are also both followed by a verb and an adjective.

Here's another one along the same lines:

Jason, who is a nice guy and who also dresses really well, visited me yesterday.

The phrases *"who is* a nice guy" and *"who* also *dresses* really well" are parallel.

## Parallel Practice

*Practice 5.*

Number your paper 1–5. From each list, pick out the word or phrase that is not parallel. You can see our answers in the back.

1. eating chicken soup
   wolfing down pizza
   drink milk
   picking at your peas
2. walked on the beach
   played in the sand
   saw my friend
   going to swim
3. kindness
   nice
   happy
   good
4. she who walked
   he who saw
   they who told
   you that did
5. the bedroom
   on top of the roof
   in the cellar
   over the porch railing

One other important point is that when you write, you can't be a time traveler. In other words, you can't change the time when something is happening in midsentence. This is especially true when you are using *two* or more verbs. For example:

My favorite things to do are work, played basketball, and see my mom.

This sentence should sound funny to you. The reason is simply that the writer is time traveling. The word *played* is in the past, but the words *work* and *see* are happening now, in the present.

Now read this sentence: "My favorite things to do are work, play basketball, and see my mom." This sentence should sound better and read more easily. This is an example of parallel construction.

If one of your verb endings is in the past, then all of them should be in the past.

For example: Martha walked to the store, ran home, and put away the groceries. *Walked, ran,* and *put* are all happening in the past.

## Parallel Practice

*Practice 6.*

Rewrite these sentences so they are correct and "parallel." When you are done, check your answers with ours.

1. Mary is an expert in swimming, in sailing, and to read.
2. Alex went back to school to retrain for a better job and learning English.
3. The cab driver shook his fist, was shouting at the lady ahead of him, and swerving to avoid a crash.
4. What I like most about my Dad is his storytelling, to make furniture, and told jokes.
5. Louise set up a business in which she made wreaths, picking berries for jam, and baked pies.

Now write five sentences of your own using parallel construction.

1. My mother is _____ , _____ , and _____ .
2. The qualities I most admire in a person are _____ , _____ , and _____ .
3. _____ and _____ are how I like to spend Friday night.
4. Schools would be a better place to be if teachers would _____ and _____ .
5. What I like to do most in the summertime is _____ , _____ , and _____ .

Parallel construction may or may not seem confusing to you. As you continue your writing, try to keep it in mind. This next section will give you plenty of opportunity to practice.

## WRITING LIVES

The last part of this unit is about writing stories. By *stories* we mean longer pieces of writing about your own life or your family history, or imaginary stories that you make up or have heard. The advantage of writing stories is that you get a chance to practice everything we have done so far and in an interesting way.

Stories have parts just like anything else.

- You need somebody or something to be the main character and somebody or something as supporting cast.
- You need to have some problem or event to keep the characters busy.
- You need to have something happen.
- You need to have an ending even if it's "to be continued."

---

### Writing Exercise

Think back to the common childhood fairy tale "Cinderella." Remember, she is the one with the mean stepmother, the ugly step sisters, the glass slipper, and the fairy godmother. (If you really can't remember it, get a copy from the library and read it.) We will use this story for the next practice.

*Practice 7.*

1. Who is the main character?
2. Who are the supporting characters?
3. What is the problem?
4. What happens?
5. How does it end?

Our answers are at the end of the unit.

---

## Story Writing Exercise

This is a long exercise. It needs to be done in steps and is in place of a journal entry. We would like you to write a story. You can make it as long as you want. We suggest you try to write at least one full page, if not more. Try very hard to include as many of the skills that we have already covered as you can.

*Step 1.* Jot down a list of ideas for stories. You can draw from your own life, from the life of someone you know, or simply make something up. Pick one idea.

*Step 2.* From which point of view do you want to tell this story? As you choose a point of view, practice in your head how it might sound.

*Step 3.* Brainstorm some ideas for your story.

Who is the main character?
Who else is in the story?
What is the problem?
What might happen?
How does it end?

*Step 4.* Map your story.

*Step 5.* Write a first draft.

Try to include good description, metaphors, similes.
Do you need a little dialogue for interest?

*Step 6.* Editing.
Find a partner. If you can't work with one other person, then do the editing yourself.

### Content Editing

Read your story out loud.
How does it sound?
What part did you like the best?
What kinds of images did you get?
Is there enough description?
What would you like to know more about?
Does the story tell well? If not what are the rough spots? How can they be made smoother?

### Mechanics

Check for punctuation—capitals, periods, commas, sentence fragments—parallel construction, and paragraphs.

Now that we have worked on writing about ourselves and our own experiences, we are going to move on and tackle another kind of writing that you will find useful. Ever wish that you could write a letter that would really explain how something could be done or how an event occurred? It's the kind of writing that helps people understand. Instead of organizing your writing around time, as you probably did in your stories, this kind of writing uses logic and examples. The next section, Expository Writing, is all about how to use writing to explain.

## ANSWERS FOR EXERCISES IN UNIT II

### Practice 1: Capitals and Periods
I lived in a field near a town in Puerto Rico. At this date, I did not have a washing machine and had to wash the clothes in the ravine or in

the river. We had to lay them to dry on the grates of the wire fence. This time I dried my clothes like I always did but with bad luck. There were bulls fenced in the field. When I returned for my dry clothes I found them scattered in the field. Some of the bulls had my clothes on their horns. Tears came to my eyes because I had lost my clothes. Later I laughed to see the bulls running in the field with clothes between their horns resembling small flags.

## Complete Ideas

2, 5, 6, 7, 9, 10 all needed to be fixed. Check with your teacher to make sure you fixed them correctly.

## Yet Another Complete Idea Exercise

We put in underlines where the sentences have been fixed.

### The Blues

Much of today's music has its roots in the blues. Blues music started in the American sou<u>th in</u> the early part of this century. The blues grew out of many sourc<u>es, </u>such as music and lyrics from African-American spirituals, and rural folk songs.

The irony of the blues is that it uses sad stories to cheer people up. Many rock musicians use the blues music style in their own writing. The haunting minor chords and the sad lyrics can be found in everyt<u>hing</u> <u>fro</u>m Chuck Berry to Led Zeppelin.

*Practice 2.*
July 1, 1863
Mother,
(1) Your letter, written May 25, just came to hand today.
(2) I don't recollect where I was when I last wrote you but I think it was Lancaster, Kentucky.
(3) From there we went to Crab Orchard, Somerset, and back to Lancaster.
(4) These marches are about 60 miles on foot. The soldiers are carrying very heavy loads and the weather is very warm.
(5) We are now near the Cumberland River, a place that is a lot cooler than our last camp, and we have shower baths, wood, and plenty of water.
(6) My troops, anxious to go home, are singing very lively in this beautiful grove overlooking the village.

(7) I had a letter from Sam and he said that John is away to the West. I am sorry that I could not see him before he left. I hope and pray to be home soon.

Respectfully,

Your son, George Browne

## Practice 3.

1. "I am a rock, I am an island. . . . A rock feels no pain, and an island never cries."

   —*Simon and Garfunkle*

   Metaphor: Describes a person who has a "shell" around them.

2. "She's like the wind in my trees."

   —*Patrick Swazyee*

   Simile: He thinks about her a lot, she moves him.

3. "You are the dreamer's only dream."

   —*Bee Gees*

   Metaphor: The person is being compared to a dream (perhaps even the best dream).

4. "She's like a cool summer breeze."

   —*Little Feet*

   Simile: The person is refreshing, easy and pleasant to be around.

5. "Oh love is handsome, love is fine. Love is a jewel when it is new . . ."

   —*Traditional folk song*

   Metaphor: Compares love to a person and to a jewel.

6. "Goodnight you moonlight ladies . . ."

   —*James Taylor*

   Metaphor: The women are only in his dreams.

7. "She is as cold as the soles of a gravedigger's feet . . ."

   —*Traditional*

   Simile: The person is heartless.

8. "He is meaner than a snake and colder than charity . . ."

   —*Traditional*

   Metaphor: The person is heartless as a snake and has no feeling.

9. "I'm a crawling king snake and I rule my den."

   —*John Lee Mooken*

   Metaphor: The person is top dog.

## Practice 4.

(1) Bertha Snoot sat on her couch, blowing huge pink strawberry gum bubbles. (2) "My life is so boring," she said to herself. (3) "Nothing ever happens to me. (4) All I do is sit around." (5)

Suddenly, Bertha Snoot heard a knock on her door. (6) She peeped through the spy hole, and to her surprise there stood a very elegant red-headed woman dressed in purple satin. (7) "May I come in?" she asked. (8) "I am not from the Department of Health, the Urban League, or the United Way. (9) I don't sell vacuum cleaners or magazines, or give away soap." (10) Her voice was as soft and silky as the whiskers on Bertha Snoot's cat, Bombay.

(11) "If you don't sell anything and aren't from anywhere, who are you?" inquired Miss Snoot.

(12) "Why isn't it obvious?" said the strange woman. (13) "I am your travel agent, your ticket to adventure and romance. (14) Just let me in," she cooed. (15) "A few moments of your time is all I ask." (16) Bertha Snoot was indeed intrigued.

(17) "What a boring life, what a boring apartment, what could it hurt? (18) I could just listen for a minute," she whispered to herself. (19) "I'll just let her in for a minute."

(20) With that Bertha Snoot opened her apartment door. (21) Little did she know that her life and her cat's would never be the same again.

## Practice 5.

1. eating chicken soup
   wolfing down pizza
   *drink milk*
   picking at your peas
2. walked on the beach
   played in the sand
   saw my friend
   *going to swim*
3. *kindness*
   nice
   happy
   good
4. she who walked
   he who saw
   they who told
   *you that did*
5. *the bedroom*
   on top of the roof
   in the cellar
   over the porch railing

## Practice 6.

1. Mary is an expert in swimming, in sailing, and in reading.
2. Alex went back to school to retrain for a better job and learn English.
3. The cab driver shook his fist, shouted at the lady ahead of him, and swerved to avoid a crash.

4.  What I like most about my Dad is his storytelling, his furniture making, and his joke telling.
5.  Louise set up a business in which she made wreaths, picked berries for jam, and baked pies.

*Practice 7.*

1.  Who is the main character?
    Cinderella
2.  Who are the supporting characters?
    The stepsisters, stepmother, prince, fairy godmother
3.  What is the problem?
    Cinderella, who is basically pretty nice, lives with a bunch of mean, selfish, insecure people who won't let her attend the prince's ball.
4.  What happens?
    Cinderella makes a dress. The stepsisters wreck it. Cinderella is very unhappy until the fairy godmother comes and saves her. She goes to the ball, has a great time, and loses her slipper.
5.  How does it end?
    The prince finds her because she is the only one who can fit into the tiny slipper. Cinderella marries the prince and lives happily ever after.

# Unit III

# Answering Questions: Expository Writing

## EXPOSITORY WHAT?

We all have questions. Many of these questions are probably like: "How do I do that?" or "What does that mean?" or even, "Why is that?" Expository writing is the kind of writing you would use to answer these questions. Quite simply, it is writing that explains and instructs.

For example, when you give a friend a recipe you have to include more than just the ingredients; you need to tell your friend what to do with the ingredients.

Just as recipes explain how to do something, writing in the expository form can also relate why something is the way it is—for example, how pollution affects our environment. Writing in the expository form covers mainly how things work, why things happen, and the process that makes things happen.

---

### Writing Exercise: Tuna Helper

Dinner is cooking, and you just realized that you forgot the tuna for the tuna casserole. The pasta is already cooking so you can't leave the stove, but you need to get the tuna for this meal. A good friend is over and would be more than willing to get it, but s/he is not familiar with your neighborhood.

Take the next few minutes to write out a brief set of directions that will get your friend from your house to the local store and

---

back. Some things to consider are: Is the store close enough so that
your friend can walk? Will s/he need to drive or take the bus?
How about getting home?

---

## Freewrite

Most of us have probably seen those "how to" books or television shows. In the same sort of theme, take the next fifteen minutes
to write a brief explanation of how to do something you know
well. It can be anything (from making bread, to fixing a car, to doing the laundry).

## Reflections

Read what you just wrote out loud to yourself (or a friend).
See how it sounds. As you read it, listen for anything that sounds
out of order. Make any changes you need and write a final draft.

---

# NUTS AND BOLTS
# OF EXPOSITORY WRITING

## Organization

As with all forms of writing, expository writing requires good organization and a strong use of details. Think of doing expository writing as
cooking an exotic dessert; you need to pay attention to the "how to," or
the chocolate triple fudge supreme of your dreams will be the nightmare dessert.

Think about the examples you just wrote. If you didn't carefully organize the directions, or if you left out too many details (whether for
going to the store or for baking bread) it's likely that your friend will be
lost or the bread won't rise.

## Exercise

Following is a section from a piece of writing that came from one of
our writing classes. We have mixed up the organization of the piece.
Read the story; then write down the correct order of the paragraphs.
Our answer is at the end of the section.

### Memories of Games from My Childhood: Handball

*1.* You must win by at least two points. You can play short games to eleven points. You can play one person, but you must be able to cover your section of the court. When you're playing singles, you can serve from your left or your right. You must be sure to keep your feet in bounds or you're out. The idea when you hit the ball is to hit the wall as low as possible for an ace. Only on a serve, a line ball is out. Other times, it is still a playable ball. If your first serve returns on the line, you lose your turn.

*2.* The game is played against a huge concrete wall. You need a flat surface and the ground needs to be tar or concrete. It would be better to have tar for the ball to have a good bounce. The ball is a regular Spalding pink ball—soft; even little kids could play with it.

*3.* When I was younger, I lived in New York City. We played a lot of games. One of the games we played most was stickball. We also played handball because it was one of the best games at the time. There were times when we played this game until dawn. This is how you play one of the games I used to play as a kid.

*4.* To play this game you need four guys: two on two. One guy serves, the other team hits the ball back, and the rally starts. You get two chances to get the ball within the square. The first team to reach twenty-one, wins.

*5.* You keep serving until you lose a point. If the ball doesn't hit the wall at all on the serve, you're automatically finished serving.

*6.* After this game, they came out with this little black ball for paddleball. You can use a paddle or use your hand with a glove. The game is more intense—quicker; the ball travels a lot faster. You use the same court and technique. Getting hit with the pink ball isn't the same as getting hit with the black ball.

## Exercise

Think of a game you used to play when you were younger. Write directions for someone who has not played the game. Pay particular attention to the organization so that your directions are clear.

## Details

Details are those little pieces of important information that help explain something or help support a central idea. Details should be as clear and vivid as possible.

*For example:* If you are making a custard and you don't mix a little of the hot milk with the eggs before you pour them into the pan, you will have a lumpy, scrambled mess (that nobody but the cat will eat). The important detail is mixing a little of the hot milk with the eggs.

*Another example:* If you are telling your friend how to keep her car running but do not tell her how to check the oil, it is quite possible that she will run out of oil and wreck the engine. Knowing how to check the oil is a very important detail.

## Exercise

Snoop around your house and read the directions on the back of common household products such as shampoo, bleach, cake mixes, and furniture polish. Write down the important details included in the directions. (One great place to look for important details is in the warning labels).

Not only do details help to make directions clearer but they also help in giving advice or explanations. For example: If someone called you for a cold remedy and all you said was "go to bed," that would not be very helpful. If you included some homemade hot drink remedy or advice on how to get extra sleep, your explanation would be more valuable.

---

### Writing Exercise: "I'm So Sick I Could . . ."

A friend has just called you on the phone. She is in bed, sick as a dog, and she wants your advice on how to beat the cold. How would you recommend that she beat the bug?

Take the next ten minutes to write a letter to your sick friend explaining what to do and why your cold cure works. If possible, take the next few minutes and compare cold cures with someone else. Read your remedies out loud to each other and listen to how they sound. See if you can catch anything you might have left out.

---

## Another Detail Exercise

This next exercise is not as silly as it may seem. There are many skills, traditions, songs, stories, and so on that have been lost forever because no one wrote them down or passed them on to the next generation. Imagine for a moment that you are the last person on earth who knows how to do something. Write a careful explanation about your skill that would guarantee its being understood (passed on) to another generation. Pay attention to detail. This piece should probably be at least 150 words.

The best expository writings do not beat the reader over the head with facts and details. In other words, avoid overkill. Include enough details to make your writing interesting and clear, but not so many as to make it boring. How much you need to make your writing clear and interesting often depends on your audience.

## Audience

Organization in expository writing (actually writing, in general) goes beyond the issue of what you are writing into the very important concern of who is reading your writing. This is called the *audience.*

It is important to remember that you write differently for different readers. For example, remember that friend you sent to the store earlier for tuna? Please pull out those directions again, because we are going to try something a little different.

In the original set of directions, at the beginning of this unit, your audience was your friend who did not know the neighborhood. This friend would need more detail than the second friend, who does know the neighborhood.

The toughest set of directions was probably for the child. You couldn't take anything for granted—what a nightmare if the kid got lost! So for the child you should have included lots of details, such as the exact number of blocks before she turns and the color of the house on that corner.

Knowing who your audience is can help you decide what you write.

## FOCUS ON "WHY"

Now we will move from the rather straightforward world of directions into some more complex expository writing.

### Exercise

This is an exercise that uses superstitions. Superstitions have a basis in belief about the way the world operates, or should operate. Brainstorm a list of superstitions: for example—"Breaking a mirror brings seven years bad luck," "Never walk under a ladder," and so forth. Choose a favorite superstition and write a few paragraphs explaining why this belief may have started.

### Exercise: "Grandma's Harley"

Your mother has dyed her hair orange and purple, bought a Harley and is going to live in the desert in a tent. She used to be this quiet woman who only baked cookies and played church bingo.

To practice explaining reasons for events, write a letter to your daughter or son telling her or him why you think Grandma has had this change in life.

AND/OR

On a more serious note, explain to a child why s/he can no longer play in his/her favorite park after dark.

### Exercise

This exercise is a change in focus. Think of a problem in your neighborhood. Explain briefly what the problem is and why you think it has occurred. If you want to, suggest a solution to the problem.

(In Unit IV we will examine the same issue from a slightly different angle: writing to persuade others that the problem you identified needs to be addressed and that the solution you suggest will work.)

These last few exercises reflect different ways to look at the question of "why." The first examines more than just describing a belief or superstition; it looks for the source or origin of that belief. "Grandma's Harley" asks you to look at personal behavior as a way to answer the question of "why." Finally, the neighborhood problems ask you to look at the question of "why" in a social setting.

Of course, there are lots of different ways to focus on the question "why." These are only a few.

# GETTING INFORMATION: WHERE DOES IT COME FROM?

## Written Connection

Up until this point, we have been working on the organization of expository writing, using and organizing details, thinking about your audience, and focusing on the question of "why."

As you have probably already figured out, expository writing is generally factual. However, in order to write directions or to focus on "why," you need information. In other words, you need to do some research. This takes a little practice.

You may remember back at the beginning of this unit when we asked you to freewrite about how to "repair a car" or "bake bread." You may not have known how to do either, so you chose a topic that you knew more about. But, what if you *had* to repair a car or bake a loaf of bread, what would you do?

## Exercise

Brainstorm a list of things that you want to know more about. Questions such as "How does that work?" or "Why is that like that?" are the sort of things we are talking about. You may also want to brainstorm a list of possible sources to find the information.

Here is a list of questions just to get you started:

How do you repair a clutch in a car?
How do you insulate your attic?
Why is the sky blue?
How do you make plastic storm windows for your apartment or house?
Why do we pay social security?
Why do clocks run clockwise?
How do you make bread?
Why is a lease good to have for renters and landowners?
How do you plan a garden?

How do you go ice fishing?
How do you start your own business?

---

## Reflections

If possible, compare your lists of information sources with other classmates.
How are they the same and how are they different?
What are the most common sources of information?

---

Many of your information sources are probably printed—such as books from the library, newspapers, magazines, pamphlets, brochures, and so forth. These are excellent sources of information. There are, however, other sources that we don't often think about. For example, social services and community organizations produce newsletters that have lots of useful information. In rural areas, Cooperative Extension has a wealth of printed material on health care, gardening, and home repair. The phone company, gas and electric service, community parks, and recreational programs also produce written flyers and mailers that can tell you how to do all sorts of things, from saving energy to making holiday gifts.

## Exercise

From the exercise you just did, choose a topic and one of the sources you suggested that uses print. For example, if you want to know more about gardening, you might look in a gardening magazine or find a book in the library. Locate that source and see if you can get the information you want. Using that information, write two or three paragraphs about that topic or write about how you got the information for your topic.

## People Connection

When you began to think about sources of information, did you include one of the most common sources—"asking others," such as relatives, friends, or even friends of a friend?

Most research is most likely done miles from the nearest library or classroom. You do research on a daily basis, and some of your most useful informational sources are probably people you work with and people you know. We are going to practice using the "people connection" as a source of information for expository writing.

## Exercise

In an earlier exercise (a few pages back), you researched a topic, using written texts. Now we would like you to do some research using the people connection.

Take the same topic you did some research on in the earlier exercise. Continue your investigation using the people connection.

Ask around to see if you can find someone who knows something about this project. Talk to them and write down some additional information.

## Exercise

You should have a sizeable amount of information by now. Combine the two sets of information you have gathered into one written piece. Three different possible ways to write on your subject follow. Pick one and write three paragraphs about your subject. (You should be aiming at writing at least 150 words by now).

1. Explain how to do what you researched.
2. Explain why something you researched is the way it is (For example, why do clocks run clockwise?).
3. Explain how someone who wants the same information you found could find that information.

## Exercise: Tying It All Together

Decide what is one of the most important problems or issues facing your community today. Locate information about the problem or issue by using general sources and the people connection. Write a four-paragraph piece explaining the situation in a letter to your mother or some other close relative. Pay attention to the organization, details, and audience. The five-step writing process could be really helpful here.

# THE STRUCTURE OF LONGER PIECES

We have been sneaking in suggestions that you write longer pieces. Sometimes writing longer pieces is easier said than done. One problem folks in our workshops often have is organizing paragraphs and deciding where paragraphs begin and end.

Organization is the key. You need to think of an overall way of organizing your work. Once the organization is in place, the paragraphs follow each other more naturally.

One way to think about this is to compare writing a three- or four-paragraph piece to building a house. The foundation, which you put down first, is the main idea that holds up the whole house. It is the biggest idea that you want to write about.

Each wall is a single paragraph that builds on and supports the house (the main idea). It is important to remember that each wall (paragraph) stands alone. Walls have supports in them that make up the frame of the wall. These are the details to support the point of the paragraph.

The roof is a summary that covers all the main points. All together it could look like this:

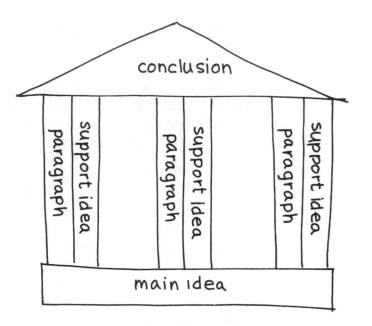

Figure 4.   The "House" Model

## Practice Exercise

A short piece on reading to children follows. See if you can pick out the main idea, supporting ideas, and the conclusion.

Pay close attention to how the paragraphs are made. In general, each paragraph focuses on one idea. However, the introduction and the conclusion include a few ideas. Think back to the house comparison: The foundation has to be strong enough to build the house; the roof has to be big enough to cover the main idea. This is not a science. Sometimes where paragraphs begin and end is simply a matter of opinion. The basic rule of thumb is, stick to one small point for each paragraph.

Our answers are in the back of this unit.

## Books and Kids

Books are magic. Kids are also magic. The combo is dynamite. Reading to and with young children is one of the nicest ways to spend time with them. It is also one of the best ways to help children learn and get ready for school. No doubt about it, reading is good for kids.

Research has shown that children who are read to on a regular basis have many advantages. They learn about language. They learn what a sentence looks like and that letters make up words. As a result, these children often learn how to read more easily than those children who are not read to on a regular basis.

When children are read to, they learn how to listen and use their imagination. Following the plot of a story helps kids learn about organization. Listening to stories lets kids use their imagination to create pictures about the action and the characters. It teaches them how to become actively involved in what they hear.

Children love to snuggle in and talk about the stories they hear and read. Talking about stories helps children learn how to explain ideas and use language. It gives them a chance to think and comment about their world. And snuggling is good for everyone.

All of these skills—listening, talking, thinking, and using language—are the building blocks of a good school experience. They are all reinforced by reading. Reading stories to children can give them just the boost they need to become lifelong readers and learners.

# More Paragraph Practice

A piece that should have six short paragraphs follows. Copy over the piece, putting indents where the paragraphs begin. Our answers are at the end of the unit.

## Why I Like My Apartment

My apartment is kind of small, but I like it. It has three rooms: my bedroom, the kitchen, and the family room. I like each room for different reasons. I like my bedroom because it is painted purple. I also love the window right next to my fluffy bed. I star-gaze at night out of that window. Stars at night are better than television. My kitchen is nice because it has a good counter to work on and has plenty of hooks for pots and pans. Most important, though, is that the floor cleans up really easily. However, the room I like best of all is the family room. I have chairs in a circle around a little table so people can talk. The television is not in the center of the room, so people don't watch it much. The family room window lets me watch people. All in all, my apartment is a nice place to live. Each room adds a little something to the apartment, even if it is a little small.

---

## Writing Exercise

Write a piece on why you like or dislike where you live. Make sure to use at least four paragraphs.

---

Before we move on to the next section we have another grammar gremlin.

# GRAMMAR GREMLINS: CONTRACTIONS

*Contractions,* or the shortening of two words into one, are easier to write than you might think. We all know that *do not* can be shortened to *don't;* but we don't all know how to write the contraction. The simple rule is that the apostrophe mark goes where you would normally put the missing letter or letters.

For example, we change the word *do not* with the word *don't.* We do this by replacing the letter *o* from *not* with an apostrophe mark. For *we are* we use *"we're,"* replacing the *a* from *are.* It is not too hard. Just remember this:

do not = don't
we are = we're

## Note: A Common Contraction Error

The words *it is* are contracted, just like above, as *it's.* This can be confusing later on when you are writing possessives. The word *its* is a possessive word. More on this later.

## Practice

Rewrite the words below as contractions. Remember, when you take a letter out, replace it with an apostrophe mark. Our answers are at the end of the section. *For example:* is not = *isn't*

1. did not
2. have not
3. they are
4. could not
5. she is
6. we are

7. I am
8. he is
9. that is
10. let us
11. it is

# ANSWERS FOR EXERCISES IN UNIT III

### Memories of Games from My Childhood: Handball

*3.* When I was younger, I lived in New York City. We played a lot of games. One of the games we played most was stickball. We also played handball because it was one of the best games at the time. There were times when we played this game until dawn. This is how you play one of the games I used to play as a kid.

*2.* The game is played against a huge concrete wall. You need a flat surface and the ground needs to be tar or concrete. It would be better to have tar for the ball to have a good bounce. The ball is a regular Spalding pink ball—soft; even little kids could play with it.

*4.* To play this game you need four guys: two on two. One guy serves, the other team hits the ball back, and the rally starts. You get two chances to get the ball within the square. The first team to reach twenty-one, wins.

*1.* You must win by at least two points. You can play short games to eleven points. You can play one person, but you must be able to cover your section of the court. When you're playing singles, you can serve from your left or your right. You must be sure to keep your feet in bounds or you're out. The idea when you hit the ball is to hit the wall as low as possible for an ace. Only on a serve, a line ball is out. Other times, it is still a playable ball. If your first serve returns on the line, you lose your turn.

*5.* You keep serving until you lose a point. If the ball doesn't hit the wall at all on the serve, you're automatically finished serving.

*6.* After this game, they came out with this little black ball for paddleball. You can use a paddle or use your hand with a glove. The game is more intense—quicker; the ball travels a lot faster. You use the same court and technique. Getting hit with the pink ball isn't the same as getting hit with the black ball.

***Practice Exercise:***

### Books and Kids

Books are magic. Kids are also magic. The combo is dynamite. Reading to and with young children is one of the nicest ways to spend time with them. It is also one of the best ways to help children learn and get ready for school. No doubt about it, reading is good for kids.

Main Idea

*Supporting Idea* — <u>Research has shown that children who are read to on a regular basis have many advantages</u>. They learn about language. They learn what a sentence looks like and that letters make up words. As a result, these children often learn how to read more easily than those children who are not read to on a regular basis.

*Supporting Idea* — <u>When children are read to, they learn how to listen and use their imagination</u>. Following the plot of a story helps kids learn about organization. Listening to stories lets kids use their imagination to create pictures about the action and the characters. It teaches them how to become actively involved in what they hear.

Children love to snuggle in and talk about the stories they hear and read. <u>Talking about stories helps children learn how to explain ideas and use language</u>. It gives them a chance to think and comment about their world. And snuggling is good for everyone.

*Supporting Idea* —

*Conclusion* — All of these skills—listening, talking, thinking, and using language—are the building blocks of a good school experience. They are all reinforced by reading. Reading stories to children can give them just the boost they need to become lifelong readers and learners.

### *Paragraph Practice Exercise:*

## Why I Like My Apartment

My apartment is kind of small, but I like it. It has three rooms: my bedroom, the kitchen, and the family room. I like each room for different reasons.

I like my bedroom because it is painted purple. I also love the window right next to my fluffy bed. I star-gaze at night out of that window. Stars at night are better than television.

My kitchen is nice because it has a good counter to work on and has plenty of hooks for pots and pans. Most important, though, is that the floor cleans up really easily.

However, the room I like best of all is the family room. I have chairs in a circle around a little table so people can talk. The television is not in the center of the room, so people don't watch it much. The family room window lets me watch people.

All in all, my apartment is a nice place to live. Each room adds a little something to the apartment, even if it is a little small.

*Practice:* Answers for contractions

1. didn't
2. haven't
3. they're
4. couldn't
5. she's

6. we're
7. I'm
8. he's
9. that's
10. let's
11. it's

# Unit IV

# *Voices Rising: Persuasive Writing*

Today you got a letter from your sixteen-year-old cousin. In the letter she tells you that she wants to drop out of high school.

---

### Exercise

Freewrite for ten minutes. Write a short piece in which you try to *persuade* your cousin either to stay in school or (for a more creative response) to drop out.

### Reflections

Look back at what you have written and write a response to these questions:

What kind of words did you use—angry words; flattering words?
What reasons would have persuaded you to change your mind if you were your cousin?
Would you have been persuaded to change your mind if you got a note like the one you wrote your cousin? Why or why not?

---

We all have disagreements, arguments, issues, and requests. Putting these issues on paper in a clear fashion can sometimes be harder than just talking to someone. Yet, writing can make your argument stronger and more understandable because you have time to organize your thoughts. Knowing how to write a good persuasive letter, article, or essay is helpful in many ways.

Writing a note to a friend, getting a refund from a company, writing a letter to the paper about an issue that concerns you, or answering a GED essay question are all examples of persuasive writing. However, it's not just in nonfiction writing that you will use the skills that we explore in this unit; your story writing can be enhanced.

## WHAT IS AN ARGUMENT?

Put simply, an *argument* is an organized collection of reasons for someone to believe or to do something. Too often, however, people mix anger and frustration with organized reasons. We'll take a look at that problem now.

---

### Exercise

Freewrite for ten minutes on something that really makes you mad.

### Reflections

Write a response to these questions. Try to share and compare your answers with another person.

Do you think it is easier or harder to *write* about something that makes you angry than to talk about something that makes you angry?

---

To write a good persuasive piece you need to organize your writing. Organizing can help you steer away from just writing an angry letter that does not persuade anyone. One good way to organize your writing is to think about the important questions that you may want to answer. We call these questions the:

## POINTERS OF PERSUASION

In many disagreements or requests, people are answering questions. The most important questions you answer are:

- Who are you trying to convince (audience)?
- What is the problem/issue?
- Why is it a problem?

- Why should there be a change?
- How do you fix the problem?
- Why will your solution work?

Use these pointers as a checklist when writing a persuasive piece. Sometimes the pointers can be used as paragraph guides. One possible way to organize is as follows:

| | |
|---|---|
| *Paragraph #1:* | What is the problem? |
| | Why is it a problem? |
| | Why should the reader change the problem? |
| *Paragraph #2:* | Suggest the solution. |
| *Paragraph #3:* | One reason why the solution will work. |
| *Paragraph #4:* | Second reason why the solution will work. |
| *Paragraph #5:* | Summarize your main points. |

How you use the points of persuasion is often just a case of common sense. You won't answer all of these questions all of the time, but keep them in mind.

## Example

For this example we return to the issue of the cousin who wants to drop out of school. Depending on the situation, good arguments could probably be made either way for our cousin. However, as teachers, we lean pretty heavily toward encouraging folks to stay in school. An argument for this opinion, using the pointers of persuasion could be organized as follows:

| | |
|---|---|
| Who are you trying to convince? | It is a good idea to keep in mind who you are talking or writing to because it changes how and what you write. Here, of course, it is a sixteen-year-old. |
| What is the problem? | The problem is that she wants to drop out of school. |
| Why is it a problem? | She will have a harder time finding a job without a high school diploma; she will need to depend more on others than she would if she had a diploma; she limits her options in terms of what kind of lifestyle she wishes to live; and so on. |
| Why should she want to change her mind? | Like most young people, she has dreams of the kind of life she wants to live, what she hopes to accomplish and the kinds of jobs she wants to have. Her hopes are more |

|  | likely to be fulfilled if she gets her diploma. Also, getting a degree later in life becomes harder because life becomes more complicated. |
|---|---|
| Solution: | We might suggest ways to help her in school (tutoring, counseling, afterschool activities, friends, etc.). Note: After school activities help folks stay in school by giving them positive things to do, and a chance to make new friends. |
| Why will the solution work? | In our culture, staying in school and receiving a diploma simply offers opportunities for a wider variety of jobs and therefore lifestyles. |

Now we can merge our persuasion pointers into our argument:

You should stay in school and get your diploma. It may be hard, but perhaps you could join a sports team or afterschool club.

You should keep your dreams of what you want to do and accomplish and the type of lifestyle you want to live. A high school diploma will provide you with opportunities for a wider variety of jobs and lifestyles. Also, as you get older, life can become very complicated. It is probably easier for you to get your diploma now than later (believe it or not).

---

## Writing Exercise

You haven't seen an old friend in over a year. S/he is thinking about making a trip, but s/he is not sure if it is the right time to travel so far. You think s/he just needs a little convincing. Using the pointers of persuasion, write a persuasive letter to your friend, convincing him or her to come.

*Note:* You may want to write a rough draft, using the five-step writing process or the mapping method you learned in Unit I. Keep in mind all the punctuation pointers for your final copy!

---

## Writing Exercise

Think of something that makes you really mad, something you would like to change. Write a short piece answering the necessary questions in the pointers of persuasion.

## Reflections

Read over what you wrote and then answer the questions below. If you have a partner, exchange papers and answer the questions for your partner's paper.

Is it clear what the writer is mad about and why s/he is mad?
Is it clear what the writer wants changed?
Is it clear how the writer wants to change it?
Does expression of anger/frustration weaken the argument?

Keep in mind our definition of an argument: An *argument* is an organized collection of reasons for someone to believe or to do something.

If there are unclear questions in what you wrote, go back and rewrite what you have written to make them clear. This time edit your work for grammar. Watch for capitalization, commas, and parallelisms.

Okay, we have looked at the importance of using reasons instead of just insults. And we have the pointers of persuasion to help us organize our thoughts. Now we are going to look at another method of organizing your reasons to persuade somebody. You can use this along with the pointers of persuasion.

## USING LOSSES AND GAINS

It's pretty simple. Two very basic ways to persuade people to do something, using reason, are:

1. *To show them that something bad will happen if they do not do it (losses).*
2. *To show them that something good will happen if they do do it (gains).*

For example, you might say to your son, "It is good to brush your teeth! If you do not brush your teeth regularly, you will probably get cavities and bad gums. Teeth and gum problems are painful and expensive to repair." You have shown your son that something bad is likely to happen if he does not brush his teeth. This goes a long way toward persuading someone of something.

## Exercise

Think of a time you were persuaded because someone told you that you would gain or lose something. Maybe it was a television commercial or a politician who persuaded you. Write a short paragraph describing the situation. Why were you persuaded? Were the reasons they gave you good reasons? Looking back, would you still be persuaded by this argument?

When you write your paragraph, keep in mind all of your punctuation pointers!

Before we get too far into this section, we should make a short note about persuasion versus logic. Successfully persuading someone does not always mean that you are making a logical argument. For example, promises and threats (like losses and gains) are often persuasive. You might threaten vandals with calling the police or tell a politician you will kick him/her out of office. You might promise a favor to a friend. You may not have *proven* anything logically, but you were persuasive.

Now we are going to get some practice examining and organizing reasons.

## Exercise

Read the two letters below. Write down the *reasons* both letters give to put in a traffic light. Our answers are at the end of the section.

*Practice 1.*

### Letter One

To the Editor:

I am writing to complain about the City Board refusing to put a traffic light at the corner of Main Street and Washington Street. We have asked them for three years now and they still ignore us. I am tired of asking! How much longer can this go on? The people of our town want a traffic light!

Sincerely,

Kim Taylor

Kim Taylor

### Letter Two

To the Editor:

I am writing to complain about the City Board's decision not to put a traffic light at the corner of Main Street and Washington. There have been over three major accidents on that corner in the last year. Without a new light, there probably will be more. Also, many children cross for school on the crosswalk of Washington and Main and are at high risk without a light to stop the flow of traffic. If the board refuses to act, we can organize and elect new members to the board!

Sincerely,

Kim Taylor

Kim Taylor

## Reflections

Write responses to the questions that follow:

How do the letters use reasons differently?
What good or bad things might happen if a traffic light is put in, or not put in, according to letter one?
What good or bad things might happen if a traffic light is put in, or not put in, according to letter two?
Is the use of a threat effective in letter two? Why or why not?
What reason would have convinced you the most? Why?

*Note:* the last two questions are opinion questions. See if you can find someone to compare opinions with about these questions.

## Freewriting Exercise

Think of an argument you had with a friend, a lover, a parent, or an enemy. Take a few minutes and try to recreate the argument in a few paragraphs. You may want to use dialogue. Look back at the narrative section for help with dialogue.

## Reflections

In the argument did you or the other person use anger and insults instead of giving reasons?

Did you and/or the other person answer the questions on the pointers of persuasion list?

Did the reasons you gave to support your argument make sense in terms of possible gains and losses?

Describe how you feel about what was said and how it was said.

## Exercise

Now go back to your argument with your friend, lover, parent, or enemy and rewrite what you wish you had said. Use the pointers of persuasion. Write a rough draft first, then a final copy with punctuation corrections.

---

## Reflections

How does the new version of your argument compare to the first one?

Is one clearer than the other? Why or why not?

---

## Exercise

You keep asking your landlord to fix your heat, but he hasn't done it yet. It's beginning to snow and one of your children has a cold. You have called your landlord three times.

List some possible reasons you could give to the landlord to fix the heat. Think about and jot down what good could come out of fixing the heat? What bad could come out of not fixing the heat? See if you can list at least two good things and two bad things. After you have done this, take a look at our list, which follows.

Your list might look something like this:

| Gains | Losses |
|---|---|
| Landlord saves money (Heat will cost more to fix later). | You will not pay rent until heat is fixed. |
| You will take better care of the apartment if he does. | You will file a complaint with the tenants' rights board. |

Now that we have our reasons organized we can put them into letter format. You may want to use the five-step writing process. Feel free to copy our business letter format. Here is our letter:

```
189 Pultney Ave.
Anywhere, NY 00000
January 11, 1991


Mr. E. D. Bloom
113 Utica street
Somewhere, NY 00000


Dear Mr. Bloom:

There is no heat in my apartment. The heat has been
broken for a long time. Since I have called you three
times already about my heat, I expect it to be fixed
immediately. I will no longer pay rent on my apartment
```

until the heat is restored. I will also file a complaint
to the tenants' rights board if it is not fixed in one
week. Anyway, it would be cheaper for you to fix it now
than let the problem get worse. Please contact me about
this as soon as possible.

Sincerely,

*Travis Cummins*

Travis Cummins

Notice that we stuck to just the points that we needed to from the
pointers of persuasion list: a) what the problem is, b) why it needs to be
fixed, and c) who our audience is. We did not need to propose a solution to the landlord on how to fix the heat; we just wanted him to fix the
heating system.

---

## Writing Exercise

Following the format of the letter above, write your own letter
to the landlord using reasons from your list.

## Reflections

Why did you choose the reasons you did?
Did the gains/losses method work for you? Why or why not?
How could you organize your own reasons differently?

---

## Exercise

You want a raise. Your boss wants you to write a letter explaining
why you should get a raise. Write the letter to get the raise.

You might want to start by listing the five best reasons for your
boss to give you a raise. Remember the pointers of persuasion and
watch the punctuation.

By now you have had some practice using the gains/losses test
and the pointers of persuasion. Something else to keep in mind when
you are organizing your reasons are the "likeliness/who cares?" rules.

## LIKELINESS/WHO CARES?

These rules are pretty simple. Most probably they are common sense.
By "likeliness" we just mean that when you give someone a reason to
do something, the reason should not be far-fetched. Anything *could*
happen, but what is *likely* to happen?

For example, if you told your friend, "You are driving sixty miles per hour in a fifty-five mile per hour zone. You could get a speeding ticket, so slow down," you have made only a so-so argument. You have shown that something *might* happen to your friend if s/he speeds, but is it *likely* to happen?

Clearly your argument would be stronger if the situation were different and you said,

"If you drive ninety miles per hour in a fifty-five mile per hour zone you will *probably* get a speeding ticket; and it's not safe. So don't drive ninety miles per hour."

By "who cares?" we mean that your reasons, no matter how likely, need to be important to your audience. In other words, how much does the person care about the gains or losses?

For example, if I say, "Put a hat on or the rain will ruin your hair," it is very likely that the rain will "ruin" your hair. However, you might not care.

## Review

Your reasons for why someone should or should not do something should be likely to happen and important enough for the person to care about them.

Try at least two of the exercises below using the Big Three rules of thumb: the pointers of persuasion, gains/losses, and the likeliness/who cares? rules. Take your time to really organize what you write. You may need to do a couple of drafts. We're getting into some tough stuff now so don't be afraid to go slowly. Write a few paragraphs, or a letter, on at least two of these topics:

- Convince your deity (goddess/god) to let you into the afterlife of your choice.
- You were speeding (you decide why) and got caught by the police. Record how you would talk the officer/judge out of giving you a ticket. When you are writing this ask yourself, "Would I be convinced?"
- Convince the sun to rise an hour late.
- Persuade someone to marry you.
- Write a letter to a politician about something you would like him/her to change his/her mind about.
- Explain how you would convince a friend to join or change to a political party.
- Explain how you would convince a friend to vote on the school budget.

We have had lots of practice by this point. You will be able to write pretty good persuasive arguments if you keep in mind the Big Three rules of thumb:

- Pointers of persuasion
- Gain/losses
- Likeliness/who cares?

Now to fine tune the skills you have been working on, we are going to look at some problems most of us have when we are trying to persuade someone. These problems are called "fallacies."

# FALLACIES

Most of us, often without knowing it, use reasons that seem good but really are not. Philosophers call these reasons *fallacies*. A brief exposure to a few fallacies can help you to avoid them and will help you write better arguments.

In the beginning of this unit we talked about people using anger and insults instead of reasons when they argue. Using insults is an example of a fallacy in logic sometimes called "poisoning the well." Insulting someone doesn't make her/his argument bad. (It has this name because in the Middle Ages some prejudiced people wrongly accused Jewish people of "poisoning the well" and causing the Plague.) It is not important to remember the names of the fallacies, but they might help you better remember the ideas.

There are many types of fallacies, most of which we will not worry about, but two of the more common ones are: (1) hasty generalization, and (2) straw man.

## Hasty Generalization

A *hasty generalization* is taking one case and applying it as a general rule. This is often known as "jumping to conclusions." For example, "My last landlord was bad. Therefore, all landlords are bad." This is, obviously, untrue. Often people are wrongly persuaded by this type of argument. Watch out for it and don't use it!

### Exercise

Rewrite the following numbered sentences and add a sentence to each to make a hasty generalization argument. See the end of the unit for our answers.

For example:

I had a bad meal at that restaurant last week.
*All of the meals must be bad.*

The last movie he was in was terrible.
*All of his movies must be terrible.*

### Practice 2.

1. I dated a woman from New York once and I really liked her!
2. The last album by that band was great.
3. I knew a red-headed guy once. Boy, did he have a strong temper!
4. I met a guy from that city once. He was a real jerk.
5. He was such a good speaker last time.

When we are trying to persuade someone, we are all probably tempted to make judgments on big issues based on small bits of information. That is the hasty generalization. Call it whatever you want, but be careful not to use it.

*Note:* a problem similar to the hasty generalization is the blanket statement that cannot be supported. An example of this is "All Americans think that . . ." It would be hard (impossible?) to prove that *all* Americans agree on anything.

## Straw Man

One of the most popular fallacies is the straw man argument. The *straw man argument* means attacking the weakest part of someone's claim instead of the strongest. (It's like fighting a straw man—it's not too hard to do.)

For example, suppose you were to tell a friend, "Don't eat that ice cream cone. It has lots of fat, cholesterol, and sugar. Anyway you might spill it on your shirt." And s/he replied by saying "I won't spill it on my shirt," then s/he is making a straw man argument. She ignored all of your good reasons not to eat the ice cream and replied only to a weak afterthought.

## Exercise

Write a short straw man response to the argument below. After you are finished, take a look at our answer, which follows.

You should wash and wax your car regularly. It makes your car look nice, helps protect your car from rust build-up, and keeps the paint from falling off. Washing and waxing your car is a lot cheaper than having to fix rust and paint spots later.

Keep in mind that you are practicing this to be better able to *avoid* using the straw man, not to perfect using it!

Here is our answer:

I don't care if my car looks nice, so I don't wash it regularly.

Our response is a straw man fallacy because we ignored all the good points about protecting the car and referred only to keeping the car looking nice. When you disagree with someone and wish to persuade them, you will do a better job if you avoid the straw man.

### *Journal Entry:*

Think of a time that you tried to convince someone of something and s/he responded with a straw man argument. Recreate the argument on paper. You can also recreate a time you may have used the straw man.

## EVERYDAY PERSUASION: ADVERTISING

## Exercise

Have you ever noticed that advertisements often do not give you good reasons to purchase what they are advertising? Choose at least five of the examples below and write a sentence or two explaining why you should not be persuaded by the advertising. See the end of the unit for our answers.

For example:

"All Natural"—Just because something says "all natural" does not mean it is good for you. Arsenic is all natural, but we wouldn't want to eat it.

"New and Improved"—An infamous example from the world of advertising! If something is new, it has *not* been around before. But if something is improved, it *has* been around but was changed for the "better." You cannot have something that is both new *and* improved.

### *Practice 3.*

See what you can find in these examples: Choose five and write a sentence on why you should not be persuaded by the advertising claims (like the examples above).

- Low in sugar
- I play with a Wilson racquet and I win with a Wilson racquet!
- The best!
- Fewer calories, same taste
- Buy one, get one free
- 40 years of service
- 50,000 people can't be wrong

- 1 billion sold
- Now, better than ever

## The Whole Picture

Sometimes when advertisers, or just people, are trying to persuade you, they do not give you the WHOLE PICTURE. A good thing to ask yourself is, "What are they *not* telling me?" For example, sometimes you see a movie advertisement that gives part of a quotation from a review, such as, "I loved it . . ." What they don't tell you is that the reviewer may have really said, "I loved it *when it was finally over.*"

When someone (or something) is trying to persuade you, it is good to keep in mind the question, "Am I getting the whole picture?" It is also very important to give the whole picture to other people. The concept of the "whole picture" ties in with the section on interviewing people from Unit II on narrative writing and the section on gathering information from Unit III on expository writing.

## Exercise

Write your own advertisement. You can write a description of a television ad or maybe just write a newspaper advertisement. You can either describe your ad, if it has lots of pictures or sounds, or write it out. You can advertise for a service or a product. You can make your ads as honest or as misleading as you want.

### *Journal Entry:*

Find a magazine and pick out one or two ads. Write down what the ad is trying to sell and then write down what reasons are given for you to buy the product or service. How does the picture try to persuade you, versus the reasons given? For example, is everyone having a great time? Do they associate the product with pleasure? Does the ad make you want to buy the product? Why or why not?

# OPINION VERSUS FACT

"No it isn't!"
"Yes it is!"
"No it isn't!"
"Yes it is!"

Ahh, the familiar argument that we have all had! People disagree on what is fact and what is opinion, and that sometimes results in a shouting match of simple contradiction. Although it is possible to claim that nothing can be *proven* to be fact, we will skip that argument and deal with everyday issues here.

## Exercise

Number your paper 1–8. Then after each number, write down whether the sentence is an opinion or a fact. After you have done this, write a sentence explaining why the sentences are what they are. See the end of the unit for answers.

*Practice 4.*

1. People with red hair tend to have hot tempers.
2. Ferraris are good cars.
3. Dogs sweat with their tongues.
4. This is a good book.
5. Driving causes pollution.
6. Drinking and driving causes many deaths.
7. We need stricter DWI laws to lower highway deaths.
8. The twenty-first century does not start until the year 2001.

In general, what seems to separate fact from opinion is the ability to prove a fact. You can prove that dogs sweat with their tongues, but you cannot prove this is a good book. Debates over opinion often rest on personal ideas about what is "good" or "bad." It's like debating whether vanilla is better than chocolate—there's no right answer (though we vote for chocolate).

## Exercise

Some people can be very persuasive in arguing their opinions, but it is a difficult skill to develop. Here's an opportunity to get some practice writing your opinions. Three different situations follow that have some sort of a moral dilemma. Pick at least two of the paragraphs and write a short essay answering the question at the end of the paragraph.

1. Betty works at the local branch of a very large bank. Even though she has worked there for a few years, she does not earn much money, especially for a single parent. Last month she found out that her five-year-old son, Jacob, has a serious disease. She cannot afford to pay for his treatment. Yesterday she started to take some money from the bank to pay for her son's treatment. She plans on giving the money back as soon as she can, but for now she needs about $10,000 and will "borrow" it from the bank.

   What do you think about Betty's actions? Write a letter to Betty, giving her your opinion and why you have that opinion. You may want to try to persuade her that what she is doing is right or wrong.

2. Tom, who is sixteen, is standing on a street corner in a mid-sized city, waiting for the bus. Tom is on his way to his dish-washing job, which he has so he can go to college some day. While he is waiting, a long, dark limousine pulls up and a very wealthy-looking man gets out of the car. When the man pulls a handkerchief out of his back pocket, a fifty dollar bill falls out, which no one, except Tom, seems to see.

   What do you think Tom should do? Write what you would tell Tom to do. Be as persuasive as possible.

3. Louis is in a bad car accident. After the accident, he needs a life-support system to stay alive. A few years ago Louis told his family that he would not want to live on a life-support system. However, Louis never wrote this down, nor has he spoken about it in the last two years.

   If the decision to keep Louis on the support system or to take him off were up to you, what would you do? Write a paragraph or two explaining what you would do and why.

---

### Reflections

There are no right or wrong responses to the exercise you just did, just opinions. If possible, find one or two partners to share and compare answers. Some things to keep in mind are:

Did you want more information than was given in any of the questions?
Did you have trouble making up your mind or was it easy?
Do you think you could be persuaded to change your mind about any of the situations?

---

## Review

Okay, we have covered a lot of ground so far. We've used the *pointers of persuasion, losses and gains,* and the *likeliness/who cares?* rules, as well as looked at a few fallacies in logic. We have also looked at opinions versus facts. In review, we are basically asking that you answer all the relevant questions (such as, Who are you trying to convince? What is the problem? Why is it a problem? What should be done?). Make sure your reasons are not out in space and that people care about them. Stick to the argument (no insults or cheap shots), and organize your ideas ahead of time. We'll do some more practice before moving on.

## Exercise

Keeping in mind all that we just went over, write on at least three of the suggested topics below (or a similar topic). Feel free to exchange your letters with someone else and help each other edit.

- Persuade your son or daughter to go to college.
- Your muffler fell off your car a day after the warranty expired from the shop. You are a regular customer at the shop. Write down what you would say to the manager about fixing your muffler.
- You need help tarring your driveway. Without bribing your friend with money, attempt to persuade him/her to help you.
- We have all probably "wronged" someone. Write a letter persuading a person you've wronged to forgive you.
- Think of an argument or disagreement you have had with someone. If you could communicate only on paper with him/her, how would you try again to persuade him/her in the same argument or disagreement?
- Write a public service commercial. A public service commercial is a commercial that is supposed to help out people. It can be about the environment, drugs, education, or anything you think people should hear about.

# WRITING A LETTER TO THE EDITOR

One of the best places to express your opinions is in the newspaper. At first this may sound too scary, but its not nearly as difficult as it may seem. The newspaper can serve as an excellent place to exchange ideas.

There are almost certainly things you would like to see changed in your community or even in the country. Hopefully, by the end of this unit, you will be writing to a paper, a magazine, or a television show to express your views persuasively.

On most newspaper editorial pages there are letters to the editor, which are usually no more than 300 words. This sounds like a lot, but many letters are shorter than that. Anyway, by now you are probably writing pieces pretty close to that length. A letter to the editor is just a short persuasive essay.

## Exercise

Read the following letter to the editor. Write down what you think are reasons to support the writer's argument. Organize reasons into weak and strong lists. Explain why you decided some reasons were weak and some were strong. Keep in mind what you have learned in this unit: the pointers of persuasion, the losses and gains arguments, and the likeliness/who cares? issues, as well as fallacies in logic.

To the Editor:

I am writing in support of the proposed bottle bill for the state. The proposal is to charge an extra five cents on each bottle of soda and beer as a deposit on the bottle. When the bottle is returned, the money is given back. This bill would discourage people from throwing away bottles, which would cut down on trash going to landfills. Less trash going to the landfills would save money and space and would help the environment.

In addition, if people do not turn in their bottles, the state will get extra money from the deposits not claimed. This money could help offset the deficit. I hope you will join me in supporting the bottle bill.

---

## Reflections

Did the writer present a convincing argument?
Was the letter well organized? Why or why not?

---

## Exercise

If the letter you just analyzed were in your local paper, what would you think? Write a short letter responding to the editorial you just read. You can write to explain why you agree or disagree. You may want to use the five-step writing process. Get your reasons in order first, then put them in a letter.

# PRO AND CON

What you just did is often called *pro and con*. *Pro* means you are for something and *con* means you are against it. A great exercise in persuasive writing is to do both pro and con pieces. It's a lot harder to write a good piece on something you don't agree with than on something with which you agree.

## Exercise

Go back to the letter you wrote in response to the letter on the bottle bill. This time write a letter arguing the *opposite* of what you just wrote. In other words, if you argued pro (telling the editor you agreed with him/her), write this one con (you disagree). If you argued con in your first letter, write this one pro.

Remember to organize your thoughts ahead of time!

### Editing

Go back to your letter or essay and make any changes you think would strengthen the argument.

## Exercise

Brainstorm a list of topics that could be debated in a newspaper. Pick a topic from the list and write a short letter to the editor for *both* sides, making the strongest arguments you can. See if you can share and compare your answers with a partner or a group.

*Journal Entry:*

Pick up a copy of a newspaper and read the editorial and letters to the editor. Try to find an issue you are concerned about and write a response to the newspaper.

## LOOKING BEYOND THE NEWSPAPER

The ability to write good persuasive letters is very important when it comes to changing things in your community, business, state, and even the country. People who organize around issues that concern them need to be able to express their ideas convincingly.

If you could change one thing in your neighborhood, what would it be? Would you like recycling, new roads, more housing, a summer parade, more police, more teachers, or maybe a park? You can always write a letter to your neighbors (as well as to the local paper) persuading them to organize around your issue. Be sure to include in your writing suggestions on how to achieve your goal.

## Exercise

Think of a problem you would like to see changed. Write a short persuasive piece or letter about it. You may want to prepare a list of reasons before you start writing. Keep in mind the work that you did on interviewing people and collecting information.

---

### Reflections

You may want to send your letter to the mayor or congressperson. You will almost certainly get a letter back. As always, read those letters carefully. Does the reply specifically address what you wrote? You may need to write another letter to follow up on any questions not answered.

---

# GRAMMAR GREMLINS: POSSESSIVES

We are almost ready to move on, but before we do we have some more grammar gremlins to take a look at and practice. This time we are studying how to spell and use possessives. *Possessives* are words or phrases that indicate that someone owns or controls something (my brother's car, my cousins' house).

The rules are pretty straightforward:

1.  When you have one person or thing that possesses something, you add an *s* preceded by an apostrophe. This is called adding an "apostrophe *s*." *For example:* "My dog's fleas are trouble" or "My sister's hair is brown." This is usually all you have to do.
    Sometimes, though, you need rule number two:

2.  When the name ends in the letter *s*, or there is more than one person or thing possessing something, we use the "*s* apostrophe." *For example*, "I have two dogs, and my dogs' fleas are trouble." When the word already ends in *s* like Adams we can say, "The Adams' car is red."

*Practice 5.*

Rewrite these sentences. Add apostrophes and the letter *s* when and where they are needed to make the possessives correct. See the end of the unit for the answers. For example:

*Incorrect punctuation:*
    My fathers favorite chair had lots of holes.
*Correct:*
    My father's favorite chair had lots of holes.
*Incorrect punctuation:*
    My three sisters cars have air conditioning.
*Correct:*
    My three sisters' cars have air conditioning.

Number your paper 1–10 and rewrite these sentences using the correct possessive form:

1.  That mans car is really cool.
2.  My mothers house always smelled good.
3.  The Temples books are always great!
4.  The old mans house survived the storm.
5.  Hollys hair grows fast and furious.
6.  Cheris new shirt looks nice.
7.  Joes girlfriend goes for cheap guys.

8.  The Williams lawn needs cutting.
9.  All of the three buildings windows were dark.
10. Toms cooking is great!

This marks the end of the persuasive writing section. Keep in mind that practice is the best way to improve your writing, especially when it comes to writing a good persuasive piece. It will also be a big help in the next unit, which is writing essays.

# ANSWERS FOR EXERCISES IN UNIT IV

*Practice 1:* Comparing Reasons from Letters One and Two
*Letter One:* The only reason that letter one gave to put in a traffic light was that the "people of the town" want one.
*Letter Two:* Letter two gave a few good reasons: (1) there have been three accidents on the corner—a light could help control accidents, (2) children cross the street without a light to help them, which is dangerous, (3) a threat to vote out the members who do not help to put in a light.

*Practice 2:* Hasty Generalization
Other answers are possible, but these are our answers.

1.  I dated a woman from New York once and I really liked her!
    *I will like all the women I date from New York.*
2.  The last album by that band was great.
    *All of their albums must be great.*
3.  I knew a red-headed guy once. Boy, did he have a strong temper!
    *All red-headed guys must have strong tempers.*
4.  I met a guy from that town once. He was a real jerk.
    *All guys from that town are real jerks.*
5.  He was such a good speaker last time.
    *He must always be a good speaker.*

*Practice 3:* Advertisements
These are our answers; yours may be different.

- Low in sugar
    The ad does not say what "low" means. Low in sugar could still be a lot of sugar.
- I play with a Wilson racquet and I win with a Wilson racquet!
    You can win with a racquet and you can *lose* with a racquet.
- The best!
    Just because something is "the best" doesn't mean it is good. It only means that it's better than everything else.

- Fewer calories, same taste

    Often the source of the taste is the source of the calories. If you change the ingredients that give you the calories, you probably change the taste.

- Buy one, get one free

    What you are really getting is two things at half price (which may be good!). However, you are not really getting anything for free.

- 40 years of service

    Just because something has been around for a long time does not mean it is good. It *may* be good, but a long history doesn't mean that it is good.

- 50,000 people can't be wrong

    Sure they can! Lots of people will buy something (or vote for someone) and not like what they did.

- 1 billion sold

    Again, just because one billion of something is sold, doesn't mean you will like it or that it is good. You could disagree with those one billion people who bought something. Also, they may not have liked what they bought, but they are still counted.

- Now, better than ever

    Something made better can still be bad. It may not have been improved enough, or at all, for that matter.

*Practice 4:* Opinion Versus Fact

1.  *Opinion:* There is no strong evidence that hair color correlates with personality.
2.  *Opinion:* What is a "good" car? Some would say a car that gets lots of gas mileage is a good car (Ferraris tend to get poor gas mileage). Others would say that a fast car that ``handles'' well is a "good" car (like a Ferrari).
3.  *Fact:* Dogs *do* use their tongues to cool off through sweat.
4.  *Opinion: We* think this is a good book, but you might not.
5.  *Fact:* Driving a car releases a lot of pollutants.
6.  *Fact:* Alcohol is involved in over fifty percent of all highway accidents, many of which are fatal.
7.  *Opinion:* Stricter DWI laws *may* lower highway deaths, but it would be hard to prove this. For example, the laws may not be enforced or may not be "strict" enough.
8.  *Fact:* The year 2000 is the 100th year of the 20th century. The year 2001 is the first year of the 21st century.

*Practice 5:* Possessives

1. That *man's* car is really cool.
2. My *mother's* house always smelled good.
3. The *Temple's* books are always great!
4. The *old man's* house survived the storm.
5. *Holly's* hair grows fast and furious.
6. *Cheri's* new shirt looks nice.
7. *Joe's* girlfriend goes for cheap guys.
8. The *Williams'* lawn needs cutting.
9. All of the three *buildings'* windows were dark.
10. *Tom's* cooking is great!

# Unit V

# Easing into Essays: Writing for the GED and Other Situations

## WHAT IS AN ESSAY?

Essays are usually thought of as being the *E* word. Folks see essays as something to be feared. Not true. Some of the pieces you have already done in this book are essays.

In a nutshell, an *essay* is a piece of writing on one subject. Usually the writer has a specific issue or purpose s/he wishes to write about. This is called the *thesis*. The thesis makes a claim about the topic. For example, "chickens make good pets" could be a thesis statement. The writer then provides explanations, arguments, and details to support the claim that chickens make good pets.

The piece "Why I Like My Apartment" on page 62 is a simple expository essay. The main idea or thesis in that essay is, "My apartment has three rooms, all of which I like." Essays answer questions with details and explanations.

### Essays and Paragraphs

Another way to think of an essay is to compare it to a paragraph. In a paragraph, there is one main idea that is supported by details and arguments. An essay is basically a larger version of this same idea. (Main idea → Smaller supporting ideas → Details.)

### When to Write Essays

You will need to write essays to pass certain kinds of exams (such as the GED). You will also write essays if you want to go to college. In college and some vocational programs, essays are a common thing. In Unit

IV, Voices Rising, we worked with writing letters to the newspaper or to members of your community. Many of these can be considered essays. Most important though, writing an essay is a good way to practice organizing your writing in general (as well as your thinking).

This unit will look at different ways to write essays for different situations.

# THE GED ESSAY

Throughout this whole book, and in class, you have been preparing for the GED. You have studied narrative writing, expository writing, and persuasive writing. You have written and edited a lot. This is the very best way to learn to write and to prepare for the writing section of the GED test.

We will give you some specific advice on writing for the GED in the next few pages, but the whole unit will help you on the exam.

## What to Expect on the GED

The Writing Skills section of the GED has two parts. One part is a multiple choice section on editing and the other is writing an essay. This book will only directly deal with the essay section.

On the GED you will have forty-five minutes to plan, write, and edit an essay of about 200 words. This is not a lot of writing. For example, the paragraph you are reading now has over ninety words. There is a pretty good chance that you have written a few pieces that are at least 200 words. The good news is that the length is not written in stone. The quality of your essay is more important than the quantity. A shorter, clearly written essay will get a higher score than a rambling, disorganized essay.

While you have to write only a little bit, you need to make sure that what you write counts. By that we mean you need to make sure you support your statements with details and reasons. You will need to organize your writing before you start. We will give you some suggestions on how to do this soon.

GED essay questions ask you to give your opinion on an issue. The topics are general and current and you are not expected to have a lot of special knowledge.

## How the GED Essay Is Graded

GED essays are graded on a point scale of one through six, six being the highest grade. Your essay is graded on how clear you are and how well your ideas are supported and organized. A few grammar and spelling mistakes will be overlooked, but too many will affect your score. You cannot have a right or wrong opinion, only a well or poorly supported one.

It is most important to have an organized essay that answers the question that the GED test asks. Too often people try to fit a generic essay into the exam question. Don't make this mistake! Each GED test asks a different question. The essay question you get is the one you should answer.

## ORGANIZING YOUR WRITING: SUCCESSFUL STRUCTURE

The most expected structure for GED writing is the famous five-paragraph essay. A good way to remember what goes into each paragraph is this:

| | |
|---|---|
| 1st paragraph: Introduction: | <u>Tell the reader what you are going to say.</u> |
| 2–4 paragraphs: Body: | <u>Say it.</u> |
| 5th paragraph: Summary: | <u>Remind the reader what you said.</u> |

### Introduction

In a nutshell, the first paragraph is the *introduction*. This sets the reader up for what you are about to say. *Clue: repeat the important parts of the question to start the paragraph.

### Body

The next section, or the *body*, is two to three paragraphs. Each one starts with *one* main point and is followed by a few supporting details. Remember paragraph structure from Unit I and Unit II? Use it here.

### Conclusion

The last paragraph is the *conclusion or summary*. It repeats briefly what you have already said. Remember summary writing from Unit II? Use it here. When in doubt and you cannot think of anything else to say, start the paragraph with "In conclusion." Remember this is not the absolute best way to begin your final paragraph, but it will get you past the GED. Outside of the exam we recommend that you be more creative than that.

**It is very important that you don't add any new information in the summary paragraph.** Think to your self, "This is the end."

## Prewriting Organization

You may not have time to write a complete rough draft, edit, and copy it over in forty-five minutes. We suggest that you do a mapping exercise to get you started. With practice, this should actually save you time.

In the beginning of the book we worked with mapping as a method to organize paragraphs. Mapping is also very good for organizing essays. Mapping acts as a sort of an organized brainstorm.

## Extended Example

A sample GED question, our mapping brainstorm, and our essay follow. For the purpose of this example we took the *pro* side of the debate. In our essay notice how the mapping form fits into the paragraph form.

*Question:* Landfills are getting full and we are running out of room for our trash. Some people would like to see a nationwide recycling program to combat the problem. Other people would like more landfills or to burn trash. What is your opinion? Write a composition of about 200 words either supporting or opposing a nationwide recycling program.

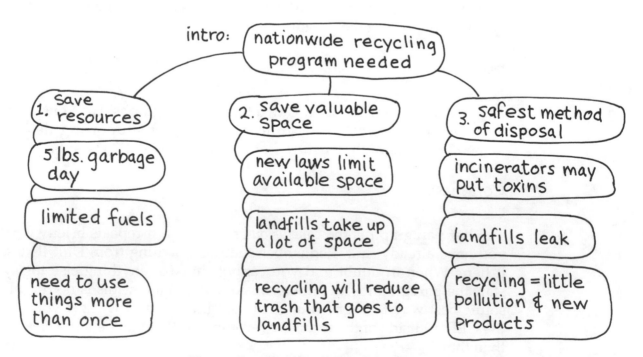

Figure 5.   Map for Recycling Essay

Now we move from the map to the essay. This essay is a good GED length (just a little over 200 words). Take note of the topic sentences in the paragraphs.

INTRO {

The time has come for there to be a nationwide recycling program for small towns. The three major reasons for this are (a) to save valuable resources, (b) to conserve land space, and (c) to protect our environment.

TOPIC SENTENCE

Recycling, by definition, will conserve the natural resources upon which we depend. The average American produces five pounds of garbage each day. At 250 million Americans this is a lot of trash. The problems with this are obvious. There are only just so many fossil fuels, so many trees, and so many elements. Using things just once simply is not enough.

TOPIC SENTENCE

Recycling will save valuable space. New and stricter laws over land-fill design will greatly decrease space available for existing and new landfills. Landfills take up a lot of space. A nationwide recycling program could go far in reducing the amount of trash that needs to go into land-fills.

TOPIC SENTENCE

Finally, recycling is by far the safest method of trash disposal. Incinerators seem to put toxins into the air, and landfills leak poisons into the ground water. Recycling plants create little pollution while creating new products.

*details*

CONCLUSION

It is evident that a nationwide recycling program can help our society in a number of ways: by conserving resources, conserving land, and protecting the environment. Recycling is safe and efficient.

## Analysis of Essay

Notice that the essay directly answers the question that is asked. It has an introduction that gives the three main points. Each of the main paragraphs starts with a topic sentence and addresses one of the three main points referred to in the introduction. Each paragraph has details that support the topic sentence. The conclusion does not give any new information.

## Exercise

Now that you have worked through one of our completed essays, it is your turn to get some practice. Following is an essay question and the map that we made so that we could write a good essay. For the purposes of this exercise we took the *pro* side. (Our essay is in the Answer section of this unit; we also use our essay for a grammar exercise later.) In the next exercise, however, *you* are going to write the essay. We will have you map and write a *con* essay for practice.

*Essay Question:*

It has been proposed that all 18-year-olds should be required to perform two years of community service. In an essay of approximately 200 words, write your opinion about mandatory community service. Give specific examples to support your opinion.

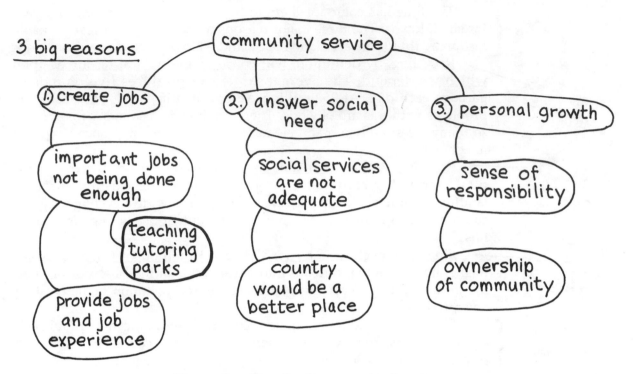

Figure 6.   Map for Community Service

## Exercise

Now, as promised, you will map and write an essay answering the same question. But you will take the *con* point of view. Here is the question again:

It has been proposed that all 18-year-olds should be required to perform two years of community service. In an essay of approximately 200 words, write your opinion about mandatory community service. Give specific examples to support your opinion.

## General Tips for Good GED Essay Writing

- Keep your sentences short and sweet. The longer the sentence, the more likely you are to make mistakes.
- Use words you know how to spell and know what they mean. Big, fancy words can get you in trouble and usually are not necessary.
- If you absolutely need a word you can't spell, work it out on a sheet of paper.

- Write out numbers of less than 100.
- Remember the $23,000 phone call from Unit II? You should be able to summarize your essay in five sentences.
- Always organize your writing.

## Writing Practice

A couple of questions follow that are similar to the type asked on the GED. Write essays to these questions. Try using the mapping method and the five-paragraph essay format. You may want to see how much time it takes you to complete an essay. Remember you will have forty-five minutes on the GED. However, don't be too worried about time for now. Your speed will come with practice.

### Essay Questions:

*1.* There has been a long-standing debate over the effects of having women in combat positions in the United States military. Some people think that women would be an asset, and others think they would be a problem. Write an essay of about 200 words expressing your opinion about having women in combat positions in the United States military.

*2.* Medical care is controversial in the United States. Some people think that a national health care system is needed and some people think it is not. Write an essay of about 200 words expressing your opinion.

*3.* The automobile has been one of the most influential inventions ever. It has brought good things and bad things. In an essay of about 200 words, give your opinion on the effect of the automobile on American society.

## Exercise

The following is an essay that would receive a low score on the GED exam. Read the essay and try to rewrite it so that it would pass. Pay attention to how the essay is organized.

### Women In Combat

Women would be okay in combat if they got enough training. Some people think that woman would be okay, and others think they would be a big problem. Women should be allowed to fight because women have every right to be there if men are there and they want to fight.

I think that women are stronger mentally than men.

A lot of women today are putting off having a family and children so why not fight for your country, but on the other hand I feel that if a woman has children she should stay home. Because if she gets hurt she will be disabled and could not take care of her children.

Women can be just as good as men are. Some people say a woman can't be better than a man in a military situation but that probably is not true.

In conclusion, women should be able to fight.

## ESSAYS FOR NON-GED SITUATIONS
## (BUT READ ON GED FOLKS)

In this final, short section of the unit we will focus on writing non-GED essays (in some college situations, on entrance applications, etc). These essays are a little bit different because they are usually not timed, don't always ask for your opinion, and do not necessarily have a specific length. Depending upon the situation, the essay questions can ask for particular information or assume that you have some prior knowledge. In any case, spending some time practicing writing and editing these kinds of essays will only improve your writing and your chances of passing the GED (if that is your goal).

Since essay assignments come in all shapes and sizes, it becomes very important to be able to figure out just what each essay question is asking you. This is not so hard on the GED because you are always asked for your opinion. However, sometimes people have problems with other types of questions.

## How to Read an Essay Question

It is *REALLY IMPORTANT* to figure out exactly what the question is asking and make sure you answer what the question asks. Look for the two *T*s: Topic and Type. *Topic* is the subject of the essay. *Type* is the kind of essay you are supposed to be writing. Look for clues in the question itself. For example:

Describe what you believe to be the long-term effect of ground water pollution.

The topic is ground water pollution. What you need to write about are the long-term effects of ground water pollution. The type of essay is descriptive.

The key words here are <u>describe, effects,</u> and <u>ground water pollution.</u> If you wrote a <u>compare and contrast</u> essay it would be incorrect because it is the wrong type of essay. It is wise to underline these key words in the question before you get started.

## Remember the Big Nine Types

These are some words that often appear in essay questions, we call them the Big Nine. Below is a list with the definitions. It would be wise to be at least familiar with these definitions as it could save you time later on.

> *Discuss:*     Weigh the arguments that are for or against an idea or course of action.

| *Explain:* | Clarify your ideas so that someone else understands your position on a topic or issue. |
| *Compare:* | Look at two or more ideas and explain how they are the same and/or different. |
| *Contrast:* | Look at two or more ideas and explain how they are different. |
| *Describe:* | Write how something looks or feels, give the reader a picture with words. |
| *Illustrate:* | Give concrete examples. |
| *Summarize:* | Only tell the high points or bare bones of the argument. |
| *Evaluate:* | Write your opinion or give the opinion of others or experts on a specific topic. |
| *Give your opinion:* | Write what you believe to be true, or the best course of action, usually you support your opinion with specific examples. |

## Two *Ts* Practice

Look for the two *Ts* (Topic and Type) in the following essay questions. Also try to pick out specific details from the question that you would include in your answer. Compare your answers with ours at the end of the unit.

*For example:* In the 1992 Olympics, professional athletes will be permitted to compete for the first time. Write an essay of about 200 words that evaluates the reasons for and against permitting professional athletes to compete in the Olympics.

*Answer:* The topic is <u>permitting professional athletes to compete in the Olympics</u>. The type of essay is <u>evaluative</u>, using reasons that are for and against.

*Practice 1.*

1. We are simply running out of space on the planet to put our trash. By the year 2050 landfills may have to be a thing of the past. Discuss some possible solutions to the landfill dilemma.

2. Some experts are proposing a "mommy track" for women in business. The rationale is that women who have children are unable to devote the time and energy that is required to be a highly placed executive. Do you believe that women in business are unable to balance family and work at the executive level? Write an essay of about 200 words that explains your opinion. Make sure to use specific examples.

3. There are many different types of day-care setups. Two of the most prevalent are: (1) a licensed center, and (2) an individual

who babysits in her private home. Which day-care system do you think is the best, a licensed center or an individual babysitter? Write an essay of about 200 words that explains your opinion.

## Practice Exercise

Go to pages 93 and 95 and select another essay topic. Organize your ideas into the five-paragraph structure. If you find them helpful, use your mapping skills.

## Editing Essays:
## The O.C.M. Method

Editing your essay is very important. This usually means you need at least one rough draft before the final copy. The O.C.M. (awesome) method is a good way to edit your essays:

Organize your editing into three sections. You want to check for *Organization, Content,* and *Mechanics.* Plan on reading your essay three separate times for each one. Each time, read your essay softly out loud. (If you have to, cover your ears to hear yourself better.)

We will take organization, content, and mechanics one at a time. This is no harder than all the other editing sessions you have done by yourself, with your teacher, or with a partner as you have worked your way through this book.

*Organization:* Ask yourself, is the $23,000 phone call possible? You should be able to reduce your entire 200-word essay to *five sentences.* In other words, you should be able to use your topic sentences to summarize your essay. The five sentences should make sense if you read them out loud and in order.

Questions to keep in mind for organization:

1. Does each paragraph start with a general sentence followed by details?
2. Is the conclusion a summary of the essay? (Make sure you have no new information in the conclusion).

*Content:* Read your essay again and check to see:

1. Are your reasons reasonable? Remember P.O.P., pointers of persuasion. (See Unit IV, on persuasive writing.) Would you be convinced?
2. Have you said what you wanted to say? Remember answering the questions from Unit III, on expository writing.
3. Make sure that you address what is needed.

*Mechanics:* Read through your essay again and check for:

1.  Punctuation mistakes—specifically periods and capital letters. Do you have any run-ons or sentence fragments? Do the breath test on each sentence.
2.  Commas—remember the detail door.
3.  Agreement—do the nouns match the verbs and do the pronouns match the nouns? Do you avoid time-traveling in verb forms?
4.  Parallelisms—are the words you used in a series written in the same format?

### *Practice 2.*

What follows is the essay we wrote from our mapping activity on community service on page 92. There are a good many mistakes. Read through the essay three times using the O.C.M. method. Make corrections as you go. Rewrite the essay. When you are finished with yours, look at our corrected version at the end of the unit.

There are many jobs in this country that, although very important, are not being done enough. these jobs include, teaching and tutoring, cleaning and repairing of parks and neighborhoods, day-care work, recreational programs for children, and working with the elderly. There are also many people who do not have jobs. A mandatory service program would provide jobs. And job experience for many people.

The time has come for this country to adopt a mandatory community service program. Although there are many reasons to adopt this proposal, three main reasons are: to create jobs. answer a social need. and provide opportunities for personal growth.

These jobs would answer a social need. Social services in this country simply are not addressing the need. Their are many elderly people who need help with daily chores. Their are children who need after-school care. Their are parks and bridges and buildings that need repair. The country would be a better place were these needs addressed. One good way to address them is with a service program.

In conclusion, a mandatory community service program would create jobs. In meaningful areas that are greatly needed. Beyond aiding in cutting down unemployment. It would help people develop a sense of community. And concern for their country.

Finally, community service provides opportunities for personal growth. It helps to instill a sense of responsibility for and ownership in one's community. A community's problems seem more manageable when one has had a role in solving them.

## Practice Exercise

Here are three essay topics; pick one and write an essay. Go through all the steps we just practiced in this section, as a quick review.

1. Read and underline key words.
2. Plan your essay map or brainstorm your ideas. Remember the five-paragraph structure and $23,000 phone call.
3. Write the first draft.
4. Edit your work using the O.C.M. method.
5. Rewrite.

*1.* The rain forests are being chopped down at an alarming number of acres per day. Scientists tell us that without the rain forests the planet may be in danger. The people who live and work in the rain forests are very, very poor and logging is their only way to make a living. In an essay of about 200 words contrast the problem of rain forest depletion and the need for poor people to make a living.

2. Driving while intoxicated (or DWI) is a common occurrence in our society. Alcohol related traffic accidents account for a large percentage of the total of highway fatalities. Many people have proposed severe punishments such as long jail sentences, heavy fines, and revoking people's licenses where a fatality is involved. Write an essay of about 200 words discussing the possible outcomes of increasing the severity of DWI laws. Use specific examples in your answer.

3. "Hugs are better than drugs" and "Just say no," are slogans used in drug prevention programs. Millions are being spent annually on these programs. Do you think these programs are effective? Write an essay of 200 words evaluating drug prevention programs in the United States. Use specific examples in your answer.

## GENERAL TEST-TAKING TIPS

People get nervous before a test because they give the test more power than it actually has. (Get real, no one is asking you to jump off the Empire State Building with a bed sheet as a parachute). Sweaty palms and panic set in as part of the fight-or-flight reaction that occurs as a response to danger. People think of tests as dangerous, which in nine times out of ten they are not. This is a writing test and if you change the way you think about it, it can be fun. Here is a chance to really "strut your stuff." What follows are exercises that will help you get rid of the jitters.

### Write Affirmations

Words are powerful things. In some cultures people believe that if you say something, then it becomes real. One way to get over being nervous is to make a list of affirmations, that is a list of all your good qualities as a writer.

## Exercise

Write at least ten and start with this one: I am a good writer.

## Visualize Success

Visualization is rehearsing the activity in your mind's eye before you do it. Visualization has become an important part of many athletic training programs. For example, Olympic athletes practice visualization before world-class competition. Major-league football teams visualize an important game before they play. What works for world-class athletes can work for you! Visualize yourself completing the task successfully. See yourself as a winner.

*Practice Exercise:* Do this the night before.

Visualizations can be done mentally or on paper. For those of you taking tests, such as the GED, we suggest the following as a night-before preparation.

## Think Positively

Write about successfully completing your test. See yourself confidently sitting down at the table, reading the essay topic, grinning from ear to ear. See yourself planning what to say, and writing an excellent essay! You are a winner. Include as much detail as you can. What are you going to wear? What are the sounds you might hear? How does the chair feel? When you're finished writing this visualization, read it back to yourself out loud. Save it and read it again a few hours before the test.

## Turn Off the Loudspeaker in Your Head!

The loudspeaker in your head is that voice that clicks in every time you start to get nervous, angry, or unhappy. For lots of people this is a very loud voice that shouts negative things in the middle of a test such as, "I can't do this," "Boy, is this hard," or "I'll never pass." Sometimes the voice distracts you from the task at hand by saying such things as, "I wonder if I turned off the iron?" or "Maybe s/he will call me tonight." The point is that the loudspeaker in your head keeps you from concentrating on the task at hand (such as a GED exam). What you need to do is turn off that voice. You can do that successfully.

Close your eyes, take a deep breath, and relax. Think for a few moments about some place that you find very peaceful; it could be a beach or a meadow. Concentrate on being in that place. Keep breathing slowly in and out. *Do this for a few minutes and then return to work.*

We hope that these suggestions will help you get over those test jitters or any fear you have of blank pages and writing. We wish you the best of luck.

## ANSWERS FOR PRACTICES IN UNIT V

***Practice 1:*** *Two T's*
1.  Topic: solution to landfills
    Type: discussion
2.  Topic: mommy track
    Type: opinion with specific examples
3.  Topic: day care, home or center
    Type: opinion with specific examples

***Practice 2:*** Mandatory Community Service Essay

Note: The order of the paragraphs was wrong and has been fixed. Other corrections are underlined.

The time has come for this country to adopt a mandatory community service program. Although there are many reasons to adopt this proposal, three main reasons are: to create jobs, to answer a social need, and to provide opportunities for personal growth.

There are many jobs in this country that, although very important, are not being done enough. These jobs include, teaching and tutoring, cleaning and repairing of parks and neighborhoods, day-care work, recreational programs for children, and working with the elderly. There are also many people who do not have jobs. A mandatory service program would provide jobs and job experience for many people.

These jobs would answer a social need. Social services in this country simply are not addressing the need. There are many elderly people who need help with daily chores. There are children who need after-school care. There are parks and bridges and buildings that need repair. The country would be a better place were these needs addressed. One good way to address them is with a service program.

Finally, community service provides opportunities for personal growth. It helps to instill a sense of responsibility for and ownership in one's community. A community's problems seem more manageable when one has had a role in solving them.

In conclusion, a mandatory community service program would create jobs in meaningful areas that are greatly needed. Beyond aiding in cutting down unemployment, it would help people develop a sense of community and concern for their country.

# *Epilogue*

Here we are—the Epilogue. A common definition for the word *Epilogue* is simply "a concluding or final section." We certainly hope that the end of this book does not mean the end of your writing. At this point, you should be confident enough to keep on going. Write to a friend, a paper, a politician, or even to yourself.

While you are writing, keep up your reading. Both open up new worlds that share common space. If you have been reading a newspaper or magazine but have been shying away from books—don't. Many libraries and some bookstores carry books just for beginning adult readers and writers. There is even a series of books out by new adult writers called "New Writers' Voices" published by Literacy Volunteers of New York City. Ask for them at your local library or bookstore.

All over the country new adult writers have produced beautiful stories, essays, and poems. Don't be afraid to join them—grab a pen, pencil, typewriter, or computer—and write. We'll see you there.

—*Bird and Matt*